Advance Praise for *Sma*

"*Smart Partners* offers valuable and real-world insights on how to create and sustain successful business relationships, from the view of very successful partners. Relationships make the difference."

—Bill Marriott
Executive Chairman and Chairman of the Board
Marriott International

"Over the years I have known Burba and Hayes, I have watched them thrive professionally and personally; they have inspired me, and I am thrilled to see them now inspire the world through *Smart Partners*."

—Ross Mathews
Television personality and best-selling author

"Want to be a smart partner? Then follow the stories and principles in this book. You'll learn how to pick the perfect partners, make your partnerships work, and create success in your business and personal relationships."

—Gavin Newsom
Lieutenant Governor of California

"Burba and Hayes share their decades of experience in making partnerships work for them in their business, as well as their personal lives. *Smart Partners* is a must-read."

—Jason Collins
Former NBA player

"I have had the pleasure of watching Jim and Bob develop an amazing business by not only working hard, but by making very smart decisions about collaborations. *Smart Partners* is a must-read for every entrepreneur who dreams big."

—Chip Conley
Head of Global Hospitality and Strategy, Airbnb,
Best-selling author

SMART
PARTNERS

To Kimberley, ♡
Through the years,
thank you for being a
Smart Partner.

Bob 😊

PS – thanks for being a "great" partner !!! :

SMART
PARTNERS

*Building Successful
Relationships
in Business and Life*

Jim Burba and Bob Hayes

SelectBooks, Inc.
New York

This edition published by SelectBooks, Inc.
For information address SelectBooks, Inc., New York, New York.

First Edition

ISBN 978-1-59079-375-6

Library of Congress Cataloging-in-Publication Data

Names: Burba, Jim, author. | Hayes, Bob (Of Burba Hayes LLC), author.
Title: Smart partners : building successful relationships in business and
  life / Jim Burba and Bob Hayes.
Description: First edition. | New York : SelectBooks, Inc., [2016]
Identifiers: LCCN 2015047074 | ISBN 9781590793756 (hardback : alk. paper)
Subjects: LCSH: Partnership. | Strategic alliances (Business) | Success in
  business. | Success.
Classification: LCC HD69.S8 B858 2016 | DDC 658/.042--dc23 LC record
available at http://lccn.loc.gov/2015047074

Book design by Janice Benight

Manufactured in the United States of America
10 9 8 7 6 5 4 3 2 1

Contents

Acknowledgments

We owe many thanks to many people who made *Smart Partners* possible. This was most definitely a labor of love that spanned several years.

Thank you to Seth Schulman of Providence Word & Thought Company for keeping us on track, drawing "more stories" out of us, and helping us get our thoughts down on paper. You made homework fun . . . most of the time.

A big thanks to all of our friends and colleagues who gave us their time and heartfelt stories. You are much appreciated: Tom Corcoran, Trina Turk and Jonathan Skow, Mitchell Gold, Elise Doganieri, Bruce Chemel, Chip Conley, Gavin and Hilary Newsom, Jonathan Tisch, Susan Feniger and Mary Sue Milliken, Ed Fuller, Brent Ridge and Josh Kilmer-Purcell, Ross Mathews, and Ivanka Trump.

To Kenzi, Kenichi, and Nancy Sugihara at SelectBooks: thanks for your insights and help through the publishing process. Working with you has been a pleasure.

And to our agent Christopher Rhodes: thank you for believing in our project. You are fabulous!

SMART
PARTNERS

Introduction

It's March 2014, and we are the first ones in line to dart into the Topfer Theatre in Austin, Texas, for the movie screening. Like hundreds of others, we braved cold, rainy weather at the South by Southwest Film Festival to see *Space Station 76*, a science-fiction film starring Patrick Wilson, Liv Tyler, and Matt Bomer. Our carefully chosen seats are high up in the back so we can watch the reactions of film critics, science fiction fans, and some other viewers who perhaps just wanted to get out of the rain. There's a good reason both of us are nearly jumping out of our seats with excitement. We are the coproducers of the film, and have poured our hearts and souls into it, not to mention our money. This film, now being introduced to the world, feels like our baby.

Okay, it's actually our second baby, and quite an unlikely arrival at that. We're not movie producers by training, nor has either of us ever worked in Hollywood. For the past fifteen years, we've been raising our first baby: the California-based Burba Hotel Network, a successful company that organizes large corporate events for the hotel industry. Along the way, we've defied the odds and also built a strong partnership as a gay couple, one spanning almost three decades.

To many people, our life together seems amazing, even miraculous. How have we managed to live and work together twenty-four hours a day for so many years without strangling one another, going crazy, or running our business into the ground? At a time when so many companies fail, so many business partnerships fall apart, and over 50 percent of all marriages end in divorce, how has *our* business and romantic partnership thrived?

Bob says patience, Jim says mutual respect, and we both say a lot of martinis. When we consider it more seriously, we realize that the very concept of partnership has been key for us—the real source of all our success. Applying a set of partnership principles we've developed has not only kept us grounded and happy as business partners; it has also bound us tightly to our customers, vendors, and associates.

Our line of work is really the ultimate partnership business: As event producers, everything we do requires reconciling the interests of disparate parties. The experts who join us on stage at our conferences aren't our employees; we can't "make" them show up or deliver insightful comments. The sponsors who support the events and the delegates who attend aren't our employees either. Yet year in and year out, they pay good money to join us because we "partner" with them to achieve mutual goals.

As fortunate as we've been in our partnerships, it's impossible to get it right all the time. In fact many of our principles came about thanks to mistakes we've made when setting up our business and also learning to live together as a couple. These mistakes have run the gamut. At times we haven't known for sure if we really wanted to partner with someone or if our prospective partner was a good choice. When negotiating a partnership, we on occasion haven't defined it clearly enough, or we've given up too much of ourselves in order to make it work. On still other occasions, we've entered into a partnership too halfheartedly, not committing emotionally to the extent required. Once a viable partnership is up and running, we've pushed too hard or inadvertently let the relationship veer off track.

We've come away stronger from all these missteps, and we've written *Smart Partners* to share what we've learned. We hope to help those embarking on partnerships (as well as those already in them) to build enriching relationships for themselves that stand the test of time.

Partnering is hard—*really* hard—but it's *so* worth it. There's no substitute for having someone by your side whom you trust, someone who over the years can help shoulder the burden of work and also celebrate the successes. Our culture valorizes youthful impatience, short-term thinking, quick fixes, and selfishness. By contrast, successful, long-term relationships require seemingly old-fashioned values like thoughtfulness, care, commitment, communication, discipline, determination, and selflessness. Invest yourself fully in a partnership, and you'll not only achieve financial success; you'll discover the meaning, camaraderie, and satisfaction that money can't buy. You'll grow as an individual—and together—as partners.

That sounds pretty heavy, doesn't it? Well, don't worry: *Smart Partners* isn't a ponderous philosophical tract on the virtues of going it together. Rather, it's a more casual, colorful—and, we hope, compelling—overview of what it takes to make any formal or informal partnership great. *Smart Partners* covers the decision to create a partnership, the decision to end one, and everything in between. But instead of taking the podium as "experts" and lecturing you, we offer a personal perspective, simply sharing what worked for us and what didn't. We illustrate our principles by telling stories from our lives as well as from the lives of a number of successful, high-profile business people we know. All along, we outline specific methods, strategies, and tools that we used to achieve financial and personal success. Those starting out will find an invaluable guide, while veteran partners will receive helpful reminders about the keys to successful partnerships.

We hope you'll read the book cover to cover, but it's also great to refer to specific chapters when you face important decisions, or anytime you need a little inspiration, guidance, or perspective. As we think you'll find, almost anyone can be a smart partner. No matter what business you're in, you can transcend your sense of "me" to create a very powerful "we." It's a matter of concentrating on partnership, committing to it, and embracing the right practices—such as choosing your partner well, negotiating proper roles, planning for your mutual success, and adjusting to overcome challenges as they arise. Fundamentally, it's about continually looking beyond yourself if you decide to share business (and life) with another party.

When you take partnership seriously, magic happens. It was our partnership principles that led us to do what we never thought possible, for instance producing a movie. Several years ago one of our informal "partners," Disney CEO Michael Eisner, shared a piece of wisdom with us. He said that hospitality and entertainment were really the same business: Entertainment takes people away figuratively; hotels and travel take people away literally. We had never thought of it like that before. "Wow," we said to one another, "maybe we can broaden our reach into entertainment and create movies or TV shows, not just events."

Some time later, while hosting a reception at our house to benefit a local AIDS charity, we were introduced to Jack Plotnick, an accomplished actor who was making his directorial debut with *Space Station 76*. Plotnick mentioned that his team was looking for someone to invest in the film and help produce it. "Would you guys be interested?" It was an opportunity we never would have gotten if we hadn't been sharing our success with others through charitable giving (one of our key principles). After meeting the production team, reading the script, and performing other due diligence, we made the decision: We were in. (Another key principle is to always go all in when sign-ing up for a partnership).

As fate would have it, the film itself offered profound reflec-tion on the nature of partnership, as well as its absence. In the opening voice-over sequence featuring Liv Tyler, a cluster of asteroids floats silently across the screen, traveling in the same direction, on parallel paths but not touching or connect-ing. Liv explains that we are all searching individually for our perfect paths, until something comes along that either brings us together or knocks us out of orbit. "I've always been amazed that asteroids can fly in groups for millions of years and never touch each other or connect," she says.

The two of us had been like those asteroids once. We had floated alone, unaware of one another's existence, until our paths collided one fortuitous night. But unlike asteroids and the characters of *Space Station 76*, our collision didn't pro-pel us into opposite directions. Instead we stuck together and became a pair on a singular journey.

Read our stories, learn our partnership principles, and apply them to your life. Discover what we have long known: We *is* better than me.

CHAPTER ONE

Do You, or Don't You?

Raul, a colleague of ours in Peru, is very well regarded in the tourism community and produces a successful conference that moves from country to country in South America. We were intrigued when he asked if we would be interested in "partnering, or something" with him. "There is so much opportunity down here," he said. "I know a lot of people, and you know a lot of people. We could really make things happen!" Raul didn't go into too much detail, but we presumed that by "partnering, or something," he meant working on his conference, or perhaps collaborating on an event like our Hotel Opportunities Latin America (HOLA) Conference, which we hold in Miami each year. We told him that we were flattered he would think of us, and that we would talk it through and get back to him. When we hung up, we looked across the conference room at each other and practically uttered at the same time, as we often do, "What would Merv say?"

Merv Griffin was a legendary entertainer, talk show host, and iconic business genius—the man who created the television game shows *Wheel of Fortune* and *Jeopardy*. He also reigned over a business empire that included a number of hotel assets, including the Beverly Hilton Hotel. He was funny, fun, commanding in presence, and a true gentleman. Back in the

1990s, we worked as contracted organizers for hotel conferences, and we had the pleasure of hosting some of these events at Merv's Beverly Hilton. As is customary at our conferences, we usually started with an evening gala cocktail reception where all the delegates could mix and mingle before the educational sessions began the following morning. These receptions were a good way for old colleagues to get together and catch up, and for new attendees to power network and make new contacts. At one of the Beverly Hilton receptions, which Merv graciously hosted, we talked about his *Jeopardy* jingle (that made him millions, by the way), his hotels, our business, and our partners. When the word "partner" came up, Merv turned to Jim and said, "Jim, if you don't need a partner, don't have one. Partners can get in the way of what you want to do."

These words made a profound impression on us. We don't know if Merv was struggling with a partner, or if he was thinking back to a time when he had made the wrong choice in a partner. We didn't get a chance to ask him why he said that, but it doesn't matter: his words hit home. At the time, we were having problems with a partner regarding cost overruns and decision-making authority, and the relationship was becoming strained. We thought we needed this partner in our lives because we were young and just starting out, and money was tight. But we were conflicted. Was it necessary to sacrifice some of our priorities and maybe our integrity in order to move forward? If we broke away from this partner, could we survive financially? Merv's words freed us from thinking that we had to continue with this partner (or any partner for that matter). They offered us a guiding principle to consider before embarking on *any* partnership, professional or personal.

We call our first step toward building successful partnerships the "Thank You, Merv" principle. We know Merv wasn't actually saying: "Don't have partners in business." He had many partners and business relationships over the years—including King World, CBS Television Productions, and Sony Pictures Entertainment—and these helped him become hugely successful (he netted a cool $200–250 million when he sold his company to Coca-Cola in 1986.[1] Not too shabby). We think what Merv was really saying was that you need to know why you are entering into a business partnership, you should be realistic about what to expect, and you should proceed with a reasonable amount of caution.

Most business people need partners at some time in their careers, especially when they're just starting out or when they want to grow their organizations. You can't always do it yourself, and even if you could, another party might bring better perspectives, skills, or resources into the mix. You may be new to a community or industry, lack the financial backing to start a business, or have some but not all of the skills needed to move ahead.

Maybe you just have a great idea and no clue how to make it a reality. Or maybe you lack confidence in your abilities or business experience, and would simply feel better with someone to lean on. You know you're great with people, but you're terrible at math and are terrified of keeping books and records. Maybe you just don't want to feel so vulnerable or alone in the adventure of starting and running a company. How cool might it be, you think, to have someone around you to bounce ideas off of, someone you respect, someone you can trust.

What Merv was saying to us, and what we're saying to you, is: "Wait a minute. Step back. Think about what you're about to do." Make sure that a partnership in this instance is *really* what you need and want. Is there a way to proceed *without* a partnership that would work equally well?"

Our friend Raul may be a great guy, and a successful businessperson. But even before we get into the task of evaluating him as a potential partner, we need to figure out whether partnership itself was a good idea.

HOW STRONG ARE YOU?

A basic question to consider is whether you're coming into the potential partnership from a position of strength. When you occupy a weak position, you may need the partnership—whereas when you come from a stronger position, you may merely want a partnership. One thing's for sure: You have to enter a partnership with either a "need" or a "want" that's compelling enough to overcome any forces pulling you and your partner apart. A partnership must advance you or your business and help you achieve the level of success you are seeking—and ditto for your partner.

Weak businesses or individuals may need the support of another to prop them up or motivate them to pursue bigger and better things. The strong may bring along another in order to bolster an already successful business, move into a new business arena or product line, or simply ease some of the burden of running a business. Having a clear and honest understanding about what you bring to the partnership and what you really, truly need helps you evaluate how far you're willing to go to enter a partnership, what you're willing to give up, and what you should expect to get from it. Knowing these things in turn allows you to evaluate whether partnering on the basis of a specific set of terms—or on any terms—is worth the effort, cost, and risk.

Look at ABC's popular TV show *Shark Tank*. The sharks, hugely successful business moguls, are looking for the next idea that will make them money. They don't need to invest or partner with the entrepreneurs pitching them ideas. The people imploring the sharks to invest in their ideas do need the sharks' money. They also want the sharks' endorsement, their expertise, and the notoriety that would come from a shark-infested (forgive us!) partnership. True, this is a "reality" show, but the business and partnership principles on display are pretty real. Sometimes all the sharks on the panel reject the deal offered, sometimes they negotiate a better position, and sometimes a feeding frenzy breaks out as they fight among themselves for the deal. Everyone on the show is pretty clear who needs whom, and who simply wants someone.

If you need financial backing, is it really necessary to bring on a partner in the business? Would a bank loan suffice, maybe MasterCard or 1-800-CASH? If you need expertise that you don't have or don't have access to, do you really need to bring on a partner and subsequently dilute your ownership or control of your idea or business? Is there some other way to obtain that knowledge? Maybe by attending a seminar, taking a class, joining a professional organization, or hiring an employee or independent contractor?

When we're approached with an opportunity to partner, we put ourselves through a pretty rigorous process. We start by asking ourselves three things:

1. How much will the project cost? Not only in money, but time and resources.

2. Who is doing the work? We want to have a clear idea about who in the partnership would do what.

3. What's in it for us? Beyond financial gain, will any other benefits accrue? And is the financial gain compelling enough?

If the initial answers are positive and plausible, we ask ourselves other questions designed to help us evaluate not merely the idea of partnership but any specific offers on the table:

1. Why do we want to partner?

2. Do we *need* a partner, or do we *want* a partner? Do we really know what those needs and/or wants are?

3. Will joining forces get us further ahead than we could get on our own?

4. Do we know the risks in taking on a partner, and are we prepared for those risks?

5. What do we really know about this partner, her track record, image, goals, and objectives? Do we respect her, or what we know of her?

6. Are we prepared to give up control, in part or in whole, of our ideas or business?

7. Are we willing to share our success, and are we willing to take on someone else's failures?

It's so important to answer these questions carefully. Although partnerships can confer great benefits, they can also pose deadly perils. Okay, maybe we're exaggerating just a bit, but entering into a partnership does place restrictions on your ideas and how you carry them out, since your partner will usually *also* want to have a say in how things are done. Once the partnership is underway, your expectations may not be realized, and you will need to know how to handle the disappointment. Differing priorities and points of view may arise that require conflict resolution—will you be able to handle that? Are you a fighter, or a pushover? Finally, while a partnership may bring you more independence in that you have someone else to help carry the workload, you may need to carry your partner's load sometimes, too. Are you cool with that?

THE PERILS OF PARTNERSHIP

The world is awash in failed partnerships. Remember back in the 1990s when supermodels got together with the great idea for Fashion Café, a New York restaurant at Rockefeller Center?[2] Founded by brothers Francesco and Tommaso Buti, Fashion Café was promoted by celebrity models Naomi Campbell, Elle Macpherson, Claudia Schiffer, and Christy Turlington. It seemed like a great idea and a great "partnership." Food and fashionistas. Beauty and Buti. What could be better? But by 1998, the Buti brothers were charged with a number of crimes—including money laundering and fraud—and the partnership was in shambles. The Fashion Café became a fashion faux pas in 1998.

In the early days of our business, we thought we would always strike the right deals and forge the most successful partnerships. While the record so far has been pretty good, we have made our share of mistakes, and they usually occurred when we failed to closely follow our questioning process. We once partnered with a friend of ours to produce a yearly, high-end, coffee-table-type magazine for the hotel industry. The plan called for us to recommend and solicit some of the content, and for us to sell "sponsorships" to companies who in return would receive ad space in the publication. In this case, each member of the partnership felt as if it needed the other in order to achieve a quick success and to fend off possible competition from the media side of the hotel business.

Trouble reared its head pretty quickly. Magazine publishing wasn't our core business, and it became apparent that we hadn't understood it very well. As a result, our phones weren't exactly ringing off the hook with companies wishing to buy sponsorships (ads). To survive, our partner had to cut deals and reduce prices with potential advertisers. We had never,

ever reduced prices in our main business once we announced them; it was a core practice of ours. Doing so now became very awkward for us. Many companies interested in the publication were also sponsors of the events in our core business, and they asked for deals on those prices, too.

We thought we had evaluated the opportunity properly, but we hadn't. Sure, we answered our usual questions of how much it would cost, who would be doing the work, and what was in it for us. All positive answers there. Green light go. However, we didn't dig deeply enough to fully appreciate the risks. We didn't really need this partnership. It sounded good, like easy money. Maybe *too* easy. We didn't think through the consequences of going to our existing event sponsors with outstretched hands, looking for money for something we weren't quite sure of. Our sponsors didn't quite get what we were doing. We figured out too late that we, ourselves, didn't quite get what we were doing either.

A lot of time and expense went into this partnership, and sadly, it didn't pan out. Yet the failure, as painful as it was, was not devastating for either party. The publication stayed in business, even if it took a bit longer for it to reach its goals. We survived too, battered and humbled by the experience. We still get the occasional question from an event sponsor, "Whatever happened to that book you started?" It's hard to answer without admitting that it didn't work out. Let this be a cautionary tale to you, and a reason to take our "Thank You, Merv" principle seriously. Yes, partnerships are great, even essential in certain circumstances. But they're nothing to trifle with, and they must be entered carefully and deliberately.

OUR FIRST BIG BUSINESS PARTNERSHIP

Our company, Burba Hotel Network, produces multi-day conferences for the hotel industry that bring together top leaders in the business. Hotel brands, financiers, banks, developers, consultants—basically, anyone who is on the investment side of the business—all use our events as opportunities to network and learn about the latest trends in hotel investing. Some of the most important "action" occurs not in the formal panel discussions, but in hallways, coffee shops, and private suites where investors put together deals worth hundreds of millions of dollars, buying and selling hotels.

When we formed our company, the main thing we needed was financial support. We required funds to run the company, and we needed companies to support the events by sending delegates and, hopefully, by sponsoring the conferences. Sponsors would pay a fee, and in return receive promotional considerations, such as their logos on our marketing materials.

This was long before crowdfunding emerged as a viable way to raise capital. Credit card debt was our friend. We were a three-person company in a small one-room office (and a borrowed office at that). Jim had a job in business development with a hotel architecture and design firm, and his employer let us use a spare office in the building, rent-free. It took several years before Jim would be able to take any earnings from the company. Bob took a token salary, just enough to pay our basic living expenses.

What more did we need as a start-up company? Well, we needed credibility in the eyes of major players in the hotel industry. Our business model called for both sponsors and delegates to pay us many months before the event started and before we could show them any solid results. We were known for having produced hotel events as a contract player for other event organizers, but not as an independent production company. We were often part of the team, but we had never led the efforts. If we were to generate a sufficient revenue stream, we would somehow have to show that we were part of the hotel business in our own right, not just freelancers who produced events.

What did the hotel industry need or want from us? We found out one night during a conversation with our late, great friend and colleague, Dr. Tony Marshall. Tony headed the Educational Institute (EI), a division of The American Hotel & Motel Association, an industry-lobbying group. Bowtie clad at all times, and precise, animated, and sometimes comical in his over-the-top pronouncements, he was a loveable character who had taught hotel management law at several universities. Over martinis, Tony remarked to Jim, "Wouldn't it be great if you could create an event that benefited the *entire* hotel industry?" Was this martini madness, or had a light bulb just flicked on?

At the time, only a handful of hotel investment conferences existed globally. These conferences may have had the word "hotel" in their title, and they may have featured top hotel industry names on their roster of speakers, but they primarily benefited the organizers—which were mostly media and financial service companies. These events were often just big commercials for the host, held for the purpose of getting more clients. For years, first Jim, and then Jim and Bob, had organized hotel investment events for others, with the profits going toward things other than advancing hospitality. We had hoped that someday funds raised from our events would go toward educating future hotel industry leaders, since this would directly connect the event in customers' eyes to a good cause, i.e., the future of their industry.

Jim had always wanted to contribute to the hotel industry in a sustainable way. Having graduated from the hotel school at Michigan State University, he was a hotel guy through-and-through. It wasn't just an avocation; it was a passion. The industry had been good to him professionally, and he wanted to give back by creating an event that would improve the industry. And so needs and wants came together for us, motivating us to create a new event, The Americas Lodging Investment Summit (ALIS), as in the girl's name Alice. (Catchy, right? It was Bob's idea. We now have a CHRIS too. And a Hot.E. Don't ask.)

ALIS would be an annual gathering of the entire hotel investment community. It would be *about* the hotel industry and *for* the hotel industry, in a way no other event had ever been. And whereas most annual industry events were conceived by an internal team at the event production company, we would create the event anew every year by gathering together executives from more than fifty different companies to determine what the event should look like. In this way, the event would reflect the industry's collective thought process. Want to know what the cutting edge is in our industry? Just analyze each year's event closely. We didn't have only one partner in this respect; we had fifty of them—fifty companies that would go out of their way to ensure that ALIS would succeed, all because in consulting them we had treated them like partners. Further, if the event prospered, ALIS would share its success with the entire industry through contributions to research, educational programs, and scholarships. And if it failed—well, then it failed.

Working as a contracted organizer for other conference producers, we had never shouldered the financial burden associated with production. This time, we wanted to own as well as produce. But again, we were a very small start-up company with a very small bank account. How would we pull together the resources to organize a major hotel event? We're talking hundreds of thousands of dollars. There were meeting spaces to book, food and beverage deposits to be made, marketing costs, speaker fees . . . And what about insurance? Good lord! How much does insurance for a three-day conference *cost*? Would the hotel we selected as the venue work with us and not require too much up-front? Would they take a chance on us? We had no history in the industry as a player that paid its bills.

Once we could get sponsors onboard and some registration money coming in, we'd be okay, but in the meantime, we somehow had to make it work. It became even clearer that we needed a partner to provide support. We asked Tony Marshall if he and EI would be willing to partner with us. EI had financial backing, it had a board made up of hotel industry executives who could be ALIS cheerleaders, and it had the ability to take money from the event and put it towards educating hospitality students.

God love him, Tony replied that they were interested in partnering with us. But there was one small sticking point. EI (and its parent organization then known as the AH&MA) wanted and needed to be "real" partners. In writing. They wanted to own a piece of the event. They wanted to be full partners.

Remember, as we say, if you need a partner you are coming from a place of weakness. We didn't have the power to negotiate on the point of ownership. We thought about it a lot and eventually decided that we were good with the arrangement. Burba Hotel Network would do most of the organizing/producing, and EI (now known as AH&LEI) would provide credibility, financial backing, and some administrative support. Because of our commitment to contribute funds for scholarships, our host hotel minimized the required deposits. Our bank account wasn't drained. We were off and running.

Our initial conference was a great success. We may have been the new kid on the block, but ALIS definitely wasn't the lonely kid. Hoteliers embraced the idea of an event that was created for *them*. Our partnership with EI/AH&MA has turned out to be long lasting—fifteen years and counting. The first ALIS attracted 1,300 delegates; the fifteenth attracted nearly 3,000. As of this writing, the creation of ALIS has enabled us to deliver over $15 million for educational programs, research, and scholarships for hospitality students in high schools and colleges. We have since expanded the ALIS brand to include events throughout the year in different locations across the United States. Our company also has partners in Hong Kong, Singapore, and India, and we're looking to expand in Europe and into South America (hold on, Raul).

WISE WORDS

In early 2015, hotel industry veteran Bob Hazard was honored with the prestigious ALIS Lifetime Achievement Award. Bob is one of our industry's great leaders, having served as chairman, president, and CEO of Choice Hotels International. He is one of the "mentors" who urged us to take our hired-gun conference work and turn it into a for-profit business model that we owned. Bob knows a thing or two about partnerships, and in his acceptance speech he said, "The most important decisions you'll make in life are the partners you chose, beginning with your life partner."

Like Merv, Bob gets right to the point with simple advice. And like Merv, Bob counsels us to enter into partnerships cautiously and thoughtfully—not just business partnerships, but partnerships in our personal lives, too. What do you really need in a spouse? What do you want? Are you willing to shoulder the risks of a committed relationship? What will you get out of it? What parts would each partner play? These are the kinds of questions you need to ask—and answer—before signing on the dotted line or stepping up to the altar. In fact, *well* before. Partnerships are serious things. It's better to spend a little time thinking now than a lot of time (and expense) extricating yourself from a failed relationship later. If you do decide to proceed, the extra clarity you possess up front will help the relationship take root and grow, increasing the odds of its success.

Of course, no amount of soul-searching can guarantee a partnership's success. And sometimes, especially at the beginning, you just have to leap. As newbies with ALIS, we weren't well versed in the nuances of partnership; we just jumped into the deep end. We never imagined that our partnership with EI would become irrevocably connected to the success of our company, the hotel industry, and even our personal partnership. But because we had thought through the idea of a partnership, and because that idea continued to make sense to us, we felt more comfortable taking a risk.

Oh, and our Peruvian colleague Raul? We don't know about that opportunity yet. We're asking ourselves the key questions, and we're thinking about if we really need or want to partner with him. Raul is well respected in South America, and we have plans to expand there. We need to ask ourselves if joining up with him will get us further than we could get on our own, and if we are prepared to attach our future success to his.

We'll let you know what we decide.

LESSONS LEARNED

* *Merv was right. If you don't need or want a partner, don't have one. Thank you, Merv.*

* *It's hard to succeed in life and business without partners.*

* *Your needs and wants, and how you can fulfill them, will determine if you really should take on a partner.*

* *Your relative position of strength or weakness will help determine how much power you have in the partnership. Are you comfortable with what you might have to give up?*

CHAPTER TWO

"We" Always Starts with "Me"

One of us, Bob, is a timekeeper. He always keeps one eye on the clock. In his mind, being five to ten minutes early is being on time. That's just who he is. Process. Timing. The other, Jim, is most likely to be five to ten minutes late. For him, *that* is on time.

As they say, "Timing is everything," but in our case, when *Early* met *Late*, everything just about fell apart. We had been living together for about a year, and an afternoon fundraiser in Laguna Beach with a two o'clock starting time was on the calendar. We agreed that we needed to leave at about 1:45 p.m. to get there on time, and of course Bob was ready to leave at 1:45 p.m. on the nose. This would leave us plenty of time to travel the five miles to the fundraiser, park the car, and arrive "on time." Of course, Jim wasn't even dressed by then, and Bob was fuming and calling out, "Let's go, let's go! We're late!"

By 1:50 p.m. Bob was pacing the floor of the little "fixer upper" we had recently purchased together, while Jim was still brushing his teeth. By 1:55 p.m. there was no way we were going to arrive on time, and Bob had had enough. He walked out the door and headed to the car, yelling, "I'm leaving, come on!"

"I'm right behind you!" Jim yelled back. At 2:00 p.m., Bob was laying a heavy hand on the car horn. Once, twice, three times. At 2:01 p.m., with no sign of Jim, Bob backed out of the driveway and left. Jim was probably still combing his hair or changing his shirt for the third time.

Somewhere around 2:10 p.m., Jim walked out the door to find an empty driveway.

Bob arrived at the fundraiser "late," and Jim went back inside to wait for Bob to return. When he finally did, the argument that ensued wasn't pretty.

Who was right? The one who wanted to be on time and left without his partner, or the one who was late and was angry at being left at home? We don't know, but thanks to this first big blowup, we learned a bit more about how each of us handled this type of situation. We were time-tested now. We knew that Jim would probably cause us to arrive a little late, and Bob would probably get overly anxious about it. We knew what to expect, and we dealt with it. Jim did his best to be on time, and Bob did his best to chill out when we weren't.

THE VIRTUES OF UNDERSTANDING WHO YOU ARE

When people ask how we've managed to stay together for so long without a homicide on our hands, we tell them that we learned who we were as individuals early on, we accepted who we are, and we made the most of it. And critically, before *we* did any of this together, each of us *as individuals* did this for himself.

Knowing, understanding, accepting, and just plain liking yourself is the foundation of a successful partnership, not to mention a successful life. You can't enter a partnership and then rely on your partner to figure out for you who you are. *You* have to have done that work before. In effect, you have to form a strong "partnership" with yourself before someone else can. As we like to say: "We" always starts with "me."

In business, "owning" your strengths and weaknesses and your likes and dislikes will help you know what to seek in potential partners. Every business needs someone to perform certain core functions, like marketing, accounting, quality control, selling, and so on. And every business needs certain skills on board—people skills, organizational skills, planning skills. As a business owner, you can't hope to be equally strong in every area. A complementary partner can help fill in the blanks by adding skills or experience that you lack. Someone who duplicates your every attribute while coming up short in areas where you also need help may not be the best partner for you. If you're too similar, you may agree on everything, leaving both of you vulnerable to dangerous blind spots.

It should come as little surprise that in our business, Bob takes care of administration, process, and scheduling. He pays the bills, does the books, schedules the computer maintenance, and works on our policies and procedures. He likes to say he is "the power behind the throne." Jim, meanwhile, is the front man. He is great with people and knows most everyone in the hotel investment world, and they want to know him. Jim is the touchy-feely one in our business partnership, the people-pleasing guy. If Jim were in charge of paying bills, we would be receiving late notices all the time (Note: Jim doesn't agree with the statement "all the time." He believes "some of the time" is more accurate). If Bob had to press the flesh all day at our events, he wouldn't be happy—it just wouldn't work.

We know how our partnership functions best because we discovered the good, the bad, and the ugly about ourselves first. Self-knowledge allowed us to set up business and personal lives that were sustainable and fulfilling. Because each of us understood ourselves well, we could listen to criticism without feeling devastated by it, thus opening ourselves to learning and growth. We could recognize our respective talents and make the most of them, while balancing out our weaknesses and limitations. Finally, we could resolve disputes and ease tensions, because we knew that both members of the partnership understood, accepted, respected, and indeed loved all parts of each other. Without the degree of self-knowledge we possessed, nothing about our partnership would have worked as well as it did.

ALONE IN THE WOODS

How did we discover these important truths about ourselves? We began, when we were young—especially Bob. Bob's early life was, to say the least, dysfunctional. Both of his parents were alcoholics; his mother died from the disease at the age of thirty-nine when Bob was only sixteen. After her death, Bob and his two siblings moved in with his father and the second Mrs. Hayes, who now had three kids added to her three natural-born children. It was the seventies, but it certainly wasn't the Brady Bunch.

Bob coped by retreating. It was the era of John Denver's Rocky Mountain High—you know . . . connecting with nature and expressing yourself, loving what was groovy and far out—you had to find yourself, man. Bob's impulse was to go into the woods and be alone. He couldn't count on his family or anyone else for stability, so he would count only on himself. That way, he at least wouldn't feel disappointed. He had read a book about a man who had lived alone in the woods of the Yukon Territory surrounded by the rawness and simplicity of nature. Bob corresponded with the author, who told Bob that he should see for himself if his dream of living like Thoreau in the Yukon was really right for him.

Bob was still in high school and too young to journey to the Yukon Territory on his own, so he talked his parents into letting him stay alone at their family's rustic cabin in the San Bernardino Mountains for a week. Bob isn't sure why his folks gave him the okay, since it meant a week out of school. Maybe they sensed he was at a turning point in his life. Maybe they just wanted him out of the house. The plan was for Bob's parents to drive the family up to the mountains on a Sunday in mid-February. The family would stay for the day at the cabin, then head back down to Orange County. Bob would remain by himself until the following Saturday.

When the family arrived in the mountains that frigid February day, Bob's heart sank. He had a serious case of cold feet—literally. There were about two feet of snow on the ground. The family had to walk a mile up to the end of the road, past empty, shuttered cabins to a small 1915-era building. Bob pulled a sled filled with provisions, including cans of Spaghetti O's and beans.

The cabin didn't have heat, electricity, running water, or toilets, so the family's first task was starting a fire in the large oil drum "fireplace" and preparing for Bob's fast-approaching first night alone. Fortunately, there was enough chopped wood stacked under the roof overhang to keep the fire going for a week. Bob hadn't thought about this detail, but apparently his parents knew the wood was there. It was late afternoon, and the sun was starting to set behind the mountains. Bob hauled a few buckets of clear, icy water up from the nearby creek running beside the cabin.

All too soon, it seemed to Bob, his family announced that they needed to head back home. It was a school night for the other kids, after all. Bob walked with them the mile back down the hill to the highway, said his nervous goodbyes, waved as the car pulled away, and then trudged the mile back up to the cabin just in time to see the sun set. The fire was still going. He opened a can of Spaghetti O's, and prepared for darkness to settle in. And then he thought, *What the hell am I doing here?*

What *does* a sixteen-year-old do for a week, alone in a remote mountain cabin with no TV? Bob had a transistor radio and one extra battery, so he listened to music for about twenty minutes at a time. He played a lot of solitaire. He read an old book that had been on the cabin shelf since the 1950s. He made sure the fire didn't go out. He thought a lot about who he was, and what he wanted to do with his life. Mostly, he tried to keep himself from panicking. When it's dark in the mountains, it's truly dark—not one twinkle of light penetrated through the trees. And it gets really, really cold. And silent. Every crack of a wood beam in the cabin or thunk of a pinecone hitting the tin roof conjures up images of some masked man trying to break in and get you. He was aware later of how sad this was—he wasn't afraid of a bear or other creature attacking him. It was other people he was afraid of.

Bob got up every morning, restarted the fire, and broke the layer of ice from the water buckets in the kitchen. He marked the days on a wood post so that he would know when Saturday—his day of rescue—came around again. He walked a bit in the woods, somewhat afraid that he would fall into some unseen hole under the snow and freeze to death. He ate all the Spaghetti O's, the beans, and the few Three Musketeers bars he had snuck into the food pack. The radio batteries eventually died, so he started playing Chinese checkers with himself for entertainment.

Bob contemplated walking six miles to the nearest ranger station and calling for an emergency pullout mission, but he couldn't bear to admit defeat. At last, Saturday had arrived. He was ecstatic. The family was coming to rescue him from his folly. He packed up the leftovers of food, which wasn't much, emptied the water buckets, doused the fire, and started the walk down the road with his sled. When he reached the bottom of the hill, he sat down to rest. He checked his watch: It was the time when his family had planned to pick him up. Bob waited. And waited. When two hours had passed, he began to panic, thinking he had made a mistake about what day it was. Would he have to walk back up the hill and set up the fire and water buckets all over again?

Since this was way before cell phones, Bob couldn't simply call his parents to find out where they were. Going to the ranger station was an option, but it was already late in the afternoon, and Bob didn't want to be walking five miles down the road in the dark. Bob decided the only thing to do was to take refuge under a tree, bury himself in his sleeping bag, and wait out the freezing night until the next day, which would *definitely* have to be Saturday.

And then, miraculously, his family showed up. It turned out Bob's watch had stopped, so his sense of time was completely off (how ironic, given how much he values timeliness today). They were right on schedule, and Bob was saved!

Everyone asked how the week went. When Bob told his stories he had to admit that his wilderness vacation wasn't the wonderful experience he had anticipated. Still, during the following months he realized that this experience had changed him. He had uncovered important parts of his true self, most notably his latent gregariousness. While he could go it alone, he was much more of a "people person" than he thought. He didn't need to have people around him; he *wanted* them around.

He also learned that he was a very determined person who could finish what he started—that he could deal with fear and not let it fester into failure.

Bob's week in the woods when he was a sixteen-year-old kid helped him to recognize his strengths and weaknesses and made him more confident in his abilities. It brought out defining qualities that would also one day help him to succeed in business and also make a good choice of a partner in Jim.

GETTING IN TOUCH BY COMING OUT

Childhood experiences like Bob's helped him to get in touch with himself, but we also both got a surprising boost in our self-knowledge and self-awareness by virtue of being gay. Growing up gay in 1960s America was rough; in fact, being gay was considered a "mental disorder" up until 1973. Unlike today, there were no road maps and very few role models. We didn't fit comfortably into larger society or mainstream business.

The silver lining was that our experiences as outsiders made us question fundamental truths about our inner selves. We're not suggesting that being gay and coming out of the closet is the magic elixir to success in life and business. Even today, prejudices and challenges for the LGBT community persist. But for us, coming to grips with our difference from others has allowed us to embrace everything about who we are, and to be better partners for it.

To make this point more real, and to provide some context for the rest of this book, we thought we'd share our coming out stories. We believe the stories speak for themselves, suggesting just how much self-knowledge can come to anyone who struggles early in life to accept a fundamental truth about himself or herself.

We start with Jim. His upbringing in Michigan was very different from Bob's. His parents, Ed and Rose, were devout Catholics and happily married until they passed away after long lives. Jim was the second youngest of four siblings, all girls. To Jim, his family growing up seemed right out of *Ozzie and Harriet*.

As the only male among dozens of Burba cousins, Jim became the "man" responsible for carrying on the family name. As such, he was the apple of the eyes of his Polish-immigrant Grandma and Grandpa. Jim's sisters claimed he got special treatment, while Jim knows that he simply worked harder to do many things better, including being better at getting parental approval!

Jim's love and need for parental approval was strong enough that at the mature age of twelve he announced that he wanted to become a Catholic priest and enter the seminary—not some-day, but in the ninth grade. Jim was captain of the Altar Boys at his local church, and he perceived that priests were always doing good things for others. Jim's parents were thrilled with this aspiration, but after consulting with the local parish priest, they decided that Jim should wait until he graduated from high school before making this important commitment. What was also becoming clear, yet unspoken, was that he wasn't really attracted to girls like his friends were. Going into the priest-hood would have allowed him to dodge the "do you have a girl-friend?" bullet. He could hide his true self behind a black robe and white collar.

Throughout grade school and high school and college, Jim sensed that he was different. As he likes to say, he was a little bit Michigan, a little bit Mary Tyler Moore. Everybody has a favor-ite show from childhood, one that inspires pangs of nostalgia any time they hear the opening notes of the cherished theme song. For Jim, that show was *The Mary Tyler Moore* show. Mary Richards, the title character, is a small-town mid-west-ern girl trying to make her way in the big city. She works at a job that was traditionally a man's role, not unlike a gay man working in a straight world. Jim was too young and possibly too afraid at the time to say he was gay, but he *knew* he was dif-ferent. Mary Richards was different too, but she succeeded in business by working hard and by showing kindness to others. She was always going out of her way to help friends and fellow employees. This lesson for young Jim was duly noted.

When Jim was twenty-five and living in Los Angeles, he met Eric, an Air Canada flight attendant who shared his

Midwestern values. Jim was smitten. He gave Eric his real name and real phone number, a first for the still-closeted Jim (who otherwise would have called himself Tom or Mike). On one of Eric's visits to LA, he overheard Jim on the phone talking with some straight friends, making up a story about why he couldn't do something with the group that night. Jim was lying about what he was doing that evening because he was afraid of "outing" himself. After the call, Jim got the lecture of his life from Eric. The theme? Being true to oneself and stop hiding who you really are. Jim sat there, listened, and took the lecture to heart because he really liked Eric and hoped that if he came out, it would make Eric like him the same way. But the bottom line was that Jim knew Eric was right.

Jim flew home for the holidays, and on that long flight to Michigan, he thought about what Eric had said. Their conversation gave Jim courage, and out he came, to himself first. For the first time in his life, Jim truly accepted himself for who he really was. The weight of the world was lifted from his shoulders. When Jim returned to Los Angeles, Jim's officemate Tom remarked how much "lighter and fun" he had become since the holiday break, without knowing the reason why. It was *that* obvious! And one more aftereffect was that Jim's career took off from that point forward.

A few months later Jim visited Eric in Toronto, hoping that Eric would see the "new Jim" and that their close relationship would finally happen. Wrong. Eric had a new boyfriend. It was Jim's first big rejection. Eric's roommate, sensing Jim's hurt feelings and that he wasn't 100 percent out of the closet yet, shared with him the writings of Alan Ashley-Pitt, which helped Jim stay focused on being himself and feeling okay with his sexual orientation. "You have two choices in your life," Pitt writes, "you can dissolve into the mainstream, or you can be distinct. To be distinct, you must be different. To be different, you must strive to be what no one else but you can be." These words hang on Jim's office wall to this day.

Like Jim, Bob lived for many years as a closeted gay. His little brother Jimmy died in an accident when Bob was twenty-four. This tragedy threw Bob's dysfunctional, small family into disarray. Bob's sister Patti had the hardest time adjusting to the loss. She was closest in age to Jimmy and somewhat of a mother figure to him, since their real mother had died so young, and their stepmother was, well, a stepmother. After Jimmy's death, Patti felt she had to get away—and she did, landing a job as a flight attendant. Bob found himself alone, really alone. His mom and brother were dead; his dad had remarried and was pretty much out of his life, and now his sister was on her way to New York City. And to top it off, Bob had a secret about himself that nobody knew.

Back in those days of the early 1980s, the Internet hadn't yet revolutionized how people met one another. If you were gay, you went to gay bars or met in some dark park. Neither of which were in Bob's wheelhouse. Another option was to place a personal ad and wait for a reply. Bob did that, and in short order he met Richard. The two hit it off and stayed together for four years. Actually, they stayed apart. It was an hour's drive apart since Richard, who was also closeted, lived miles away. He had been married and had a daughter, and he lived in fear that his secret would be discovered and he would lose visitation rights. So Bob saw Richard about once a week, or twice if he was lucky.

Bob had found someone to love and who said he loved him back. It didn't matter that Richard didn't want to be seen with Bob anywhere. There were no holidays together, either, because Richard spent time with his daughter. The occasional weekend away was arranged, and that was fun. They had no gay friends, because then they might be found out. Once while Bob and Richard were away on a weekend trip, Richard pointed to an obviously gay couple who were dressed somewhat alike, and said, "I don't ever want to look like those guys. We can never dress alike." *Okay* . . . Bob thought.

Bob was content with the arrangement until Richard suddenly announced that he wanted to date other people. It was over; Bob had been dumped! What a backwards relationship this had been for him. Usually a person comes out of the closet and *then* finds a partner. This time, the partner came first. So now Bob found himself back in the closet alone. But Bob now knew he had to live truthfully. He needed to come out.

Bob placed a hysterical late night call to his sister Patti. She had always "suspected" he was gay, but Bob always denied it. Now he told her the truth. Patti was understanding and said the family always knew this. The weight was lifted, the curtain was raised, and Bob's life as an "out," gay man could begin. Breaking up with Richard had been devastating, but it was the best thing that ever happened to Bob. He was free to start down the path that eventually led him to Jim.

We both learned that when you are true to yourself, you'll be at your best, and then, and only then, can you offer your best to potential partners. You should expect business partners to be true to themselves, too. After all, you will want to know their true selves, what they stand for, what they love and hate. And you can't know it unless *they* know it first.

LOOKING HARDER AT THE REAL YOU

Let's suppose you have "found" yourself in the most basic sense, and accepted the human being that you are. Now what happens? To be a good partner and to find the right partner, you need to go even further to understand yourself, your affinities, your personality traits, and so forth. Let's start with the affinities.

When you wake up for work, what can you *not wait* to tackle that day? What gives you the most satisfaction? Is it pitching people for new work, creating new products, marketing, working with numbers? Now let's take the opposite approach. Do you have a grip on your gripes? Gripes can get in the way of a successful partnership. You need to be aware of the things that really bother you and deal with them so that you can reduce their disruptive power. You don't want to join up with a partner who ticks you off by checking too many boxes on your "gripe" list. You can probably put up with some annoyances, but there is always a limit.

The two of us have some frequent gripes, including some about each other. Jim is late and Bob doesn't like it. Bob can make little issues into big ones, and that annoys Jim. We both don't like it when people are so self-absorbed that they seem to disregard how their actions impact others. Bob doesn't like the "everyone's a winner" attitude that is prevalent today. Jim has a real problem with indecisive people. Fortunately, neither of us gets too upset about any of these gripes. While the complaints we have about one another put each of us off, they don't do so to an extent that would threaten the relationship. This is yet another reason our partnership has endured.

Now let's switch gears again and take a look at motivations. The goal of any partnership should be to succeed; what partnership was ever created in order to fail? But this leaves us with the question of how to *define* success. A strange word: success. It has so many different meanings. How do you think about it, exactly? For *you*, is it about the following?

+ **Economic Power.** Does success to you mean making lots of money?

+ **Political Power.** Does success to you mean being able to control a market or capture a large enough share of your market to wield influence and power?

✦ **Market Leadership.** Does success for you mean that your business or product is the best in the market, the one everyone else aspires to be? Do you want to always be ahead of the curve?

✦ **Social Acceptability.** Is success for you about ego? Do you want to be better than everyone else at what you do so that you will achieve greater social status? Be honest.

✦ **Spiritual Fulfillment.** Is success about living in tune with your deeper purpose, about being able to make a difference in your community, which is something money can't buy?

✦ **A Lasting Legacy.** Is success about leaving something behind that will live on long after you are gone?

✦ **Freedom.** Is success about having the ability to call all the shots in your life, to do exactly what you want to do?

And finally, is success for you all of the above? None of the above? Whatever your answer is, your definition of success should align well with your partner's; otherwise, you might find yourselves running at cross-purposes. A business run by someone who aims to make a lot of money is going to be very different from one run by someone who aspires to have spiritual fulfillment. Also keep in mind that your definition of success will change over time, and that it's best to check in periodically with your partner on this issue. As we learned more about ourselves as individuals and as a couple, our definition of success morphed over the years from "making enough money to pay the bills" to "being as happy as we can be and finding ways to make a difference in our community." But it's a change that we both came to together—as partners.

MAN UP—AND BE AUTHENTIC!

In his hilarious book *Man Up! Tales of My Delusional Self-Confidence*, our friend Ross Mathews talks about his early life, his adventures of finding and accepting his true self, and how he made the most of who he is to get where he is today.[3] Ross started his career on *The Tonight Show with Jay Leno* as "the intern." Now he is a host on E! Entertainment, a best-selling author, a successful entertainer, hysterically funny, very smart, very driven, and Gwyneth Paltrow's bestie. You'll see him bedecked in his finest formal wear on all the major award show red carpets, talking about who is doing what, and asking, "Who are you wearing?"

In his book, Ross is very candid, in his giddy and sometimes raunchy way, about his childhood knowledge that he was different from most people. He talks about his desire to accept himself as someone who possesses "a voice that could be mistaken for a clown on helium." He also talks about his first encounter with "lady bits," but that's probably veering too far off-topic. From the age of ten, Ross knew he was destined to be a TV star. It took him a while to "man up" and let his true self shine through—the self we see today on TV, the self that millions of his fans enjoy, the self that his life partner Salvador loves. And thank goodness he did.

Today, Ross knows all the great things that can happen when you discover your authentic self, embrace that person, and make the most of the qualities you were born with. As he says: "You are what you are, and the sooner you stop hating what makes you unique and start celebrating it and using it to make you stand out from the crowd, the better your life will be."

You don't need to change who you are in order to achieve your dreams. You just need to *accept* who you are and find your uniqueness, so that you can live authentically . . . and be that fabulous partner you were meant to be.

LESSONS LEARNED

* *Where you came from will help determine where you are going. Learn from and embrace your past as the foundation for your present partnership.*

* *Accepting who you are is perhaps the most important step in becoming a strong "me," which in turn will help create a strong "we."*

* *Live authentically. Being truthful about your identity is crucial if your partnership is to be based on honesty, respect, and mutual trust.*

* *How **you** define success is crucial, and so is making sure that you and your partner are working toward the same, or complementary, goals.*

CHAPTER THREE

Pick a Perfect Partner

Let's be clear: There is no "perfect" partner. Great partners? Yes. Indispensible partners? Yes. Perfect partners? Uh-uh. Everybody has his or her flaws and weaknesses. So the question, once you've decided to pursue a partnership, is how to find the *best* partner for your specific situation. How do you choose a partner who, despite all the inevitable conflicts and moments of tension you may experience, inspires you to look back years later and say, "Jeez, she really was the perfect partner for me?"

There's something you definitely *shouldn't* do. Don't go in blind, choosing your partner at random. And if someone has sought you out, don't become so flattered that you jump right in and say, figuratively or literally, "Marry me!" Many people let their egos get the best of them in this situation, and they pay the price.

In 2014 some friends in Mexico who, like us, had a business organizing events, approached us about merging our companies and becoming partners. We were flattered that people whom we respected and admired would want to join fortunes with us. On the surface, the idea of collaborating felt right. Our friends produced a product that didn't compete with ours and that could have led us into new markets. They had a good reputation, they seemed to really want to work with us, and we all envisioned a close collaboration. We hired a third party analyst to help us evaluate the deal. From a purely strategic standpoint, it became pretty clear that we should pass; virtually all of the events these friends ran covered industries or topics unrelated to our own existing portfolio of events. If we added these events to our portfolio, we could easily get distracted from our core business. We run a lean and efficient company and we didn't have the extra management resources we would have needed to integrate our friends' business.

We passed on the deal, but not as quickly as we should have. In retrospect, we didn't ask all the right questions from the outset, and this led us to waste time and money evaluating the deal. Within months after we declined their offer, we heard surprising news: one of these friends, the one we were closest to, sold his share of the business to his partner. He was gone—done. Apparently, he had wanted to leave the business for some time, and he and his partner had been looking for an easy exit. They had approached us hoping to sell the business and offload it to us, and it was likely not their intention to partner with us in the way we had assumed. We had missed this entirely. We had been so flattered by their attention that we didn't probe deeply enough. For instance, we didn't ask questions when we heard that they were going to relocate the business unit responsible for their events to a separate space *away* from their offices. That should have been a warning sign, but it wasn't.

When it comes to forming partnerships, everything is not always as it seems. You have to ask questions—critical, probing questions—to understand what you're getting into. You have to compare your prospective partners to others out there, and even if they do compare favorably, you have to think long and hard about whether you're comfortable with everything your prospective partner brings to the table. You have to actively *pick* a partner, not just latch on to one who happens to come along. This means keeping a critical distance for a while, allowing time for the most relevant and useful facts to shake out.

LET THE INTERROGATION BEGIN

You would think that we would have known all this already. Our personal partnership only got started once one of us, Bob, had thoroughly and memorably interrogated the other. We were first introduced to each other one night in 1990 at a black-tie dinner at the Disneyland Hotel benefitting the Orange County Gay and Lesbian Center. Bob was with a gaggle of his friends, Jim was with his own posse. The after-party—one hundred people crammed into a tiny, one-bedroom hotel suite—was where the connection happened. Bob sauntered over to Jim standing at the bar and said, "Hi, have we met before?"

Jim shot him a bemused look and said, "No." He turned on his heels, not high ones mind you, and walked away. But then Jim, with his posse snapping him back into reality, realized that Bob was "kinda cute." So some time later, he went back over to Bob and struck up a conversation. In Jim's defense, the champagne was flowing, and so initially he hadn't been seeing things as clearly as he usually does. (He and his friends were drinking champagne out of someone's very fancy pair of Gucci loafers. But we digress.)

For the rest of the evening, Bob pummeled Jim with questions, not because he was upset at having been initially rebuffed, but because he has always liked to find out everything he can about people who interest him. His queries were wide-ranging: Where did Jim work? Did he have brothers and sisters? When did he come out? What kind of car did he drive? (Bob asked that last question because a psychic had told him he was going to meet somebody who drove a Mercedes.

Sure enough, Jim drove a Mercedes. The psychic also said that Bob's future partner would be in the hotel business. Sure enough, Jim was in the hotel business. Ding, ding, ding.) And Bob's questions continued: What did Jim like to do on weekends? Where did he live? Where did he go to school?

Jim answered every question, and asked some of his own—in fact, he asked two. What was Bob's name, and where did he live? Remember, the champagne was flowing. Toward the end of the evening, as Bob was still checking off items on the list of things he wanted to know, Jim asked him if he'd go home with him. "Those friends you're with—I'll give you $20 and you can send them home in a cab."

"No, I can't do that," Bob replied. Integrity.

The next day, Jim called and apologized for being too forward. The day after that, we went on our first real date, and guess what? Bob knew everything about Jim, but Jim knew hardly anything about Bob. That was okay. Jim had plenty of time over the ensuing weeks and months to make up for lost ground.

One reason Bob had asked so many questions that first night was that he didn't want to talk much about himself, especially his rough childhood. Bob really liked Jim and was afraid that information about his dysfunctional family would expose him as a "flawed" or "weak" partner, scaring Jim away. Eventually, Bob felt comfortable enough to tell Jim his story. He proclaimed afterward, "This is the whole package. Accept me or reject me." Rather than scaring Jim away, Bob's honesty made all the difference. It was a turning point, the moment when Jim said to himself, "Okay, I'm ready to commit."

Strong business partnerships tend to unfold in this way. No, they don't necessarily involve after-parties, but there is usually a trial period in which two parties get to know one another, test one another out, and ask the relevant questions. Hewlett-

Packard founders Bill Hewlett and David Packard first bonded while taking a two-week camping trip together. Only after four years had passed did the two begin working part-time together to develop a product. A year after that, the two formally became partners, "flipping a coin to decide their start-up's name."[4]

Elise Doganieri, co-creator and executive producer of the multi Emmy-winning TV show *The Amazing Race* along with her romantic partner Bertram Van Munster, told us that the two "had a very slow buildup" to their relationship over time, living on opposite coasts for a couple of years before moving in together and starting their business. "I think if people become friends first [before partners], and you actually like one another as a person, you have a much greater chance of success. I see a lot of people that do well on *The Amazing Race* that really enjoy one another's company, are kind to one another, and know one another well."[5]

Take your time through the trial period. Often the really deep truths don't come out right away. In business situations, people are often like Bob during the courting process: they don't talk about all the warts, all the dysfunction. Every company is going to have its weaknesses and strengths, and even when you start "dating," you're still focused on showing your best side, attracting the other party's interest. Give a prospective partner time to let his or her guard down, and give yourself time to let *your* guard down with them. Only when you reach a point of mutual honesty will you really feel good about taking a risk and joining forces. Mutual honesty is the foundation on which trust in a partnership can flourish.

You might object that you can't allow yourself the same kind of "trial period" in business that you can in a dating context. Business opportunities don't last forever; you need to act decisively and commit before it's too late. True, but there often are ways to minimize your initial commitment and engineer trial periods that let you try out the other party.

In 2008, Google called asking whether we'd like to partner to create a new kind of industry event that would inform hotel owners about new trends in the digital world. We would draw on our global database of owners in the hotel business to help generate demand for the event, and we'd also do a lot of heavy lifting to put together the logistics of the event; Google would take the lead in creating the content. Talk about flattering: We were just a little pee-pod of a company, and *Google* was seeking *us* out. Our answer? "When do we start?"

We planned to create a series of half-day events to be held around the country, with the beta-test first event held in Google's Manhattan offices in 2008. On the face of it, that first event was a success. Everybody seemed to like the content, and we managed to deliver a respectable crowd despite the challenges in explaining to people why they should attend. But we never did the event a second time. Neither we nor Google approached the other and said, "We're no longer interested in partnering with you." Rather, the relationship just seemed to fizzle out. In retrospect, the event was way ahead of its time (with credit going to the forward thinking execs at Google). It took so much hard work to put it together, and we came away feeling that the results hadn't justified the effort. As great as the content was, it didn't feel like the hotel people in attendance were ready for Google's insights and perspectives.

Fortunately, we were both free to walk away; we had only agreed to a one-time experiment. If we hadn't believed so much in taking our time to "test out" prospective partners, we might have jumped right in and signed up to do a dozen or a lifetime series of events. Thank goodness we didn't. A one-time experiment, with an option to do additional events, made so much more sense. And in agreeing in writing to do that one event, we also took steps to minimize our risk. We retained control over key issues having a bearing on how we fulfilled our obligations, and, most importantly, we retained control over our database of hotel industry leaders around the world.

In the end, we went on a date with Google. It was a prolonged date, lasting for several months as we worked on the event. During this time, we got to know one another and evaluate whether we were well matched for a long-term relationship. It turned out we did like each other, but didn't have much in common at that particular time. That's okay. It was a learning experience. No harm, no foul.

DON'T SLEEP AROUND

It's possible to take trial periods too far. Some people in business content themselves with "sleeping around," jumping from partner to partner and never settling down. Someone we know—we'll call her "Miss R."—is notorious for this. Miss R. once approached us and expressed deep interest in partnering on an event. Three months later, we found out she was working with someone else on a similar event. Three months after that, we learned she had dumped that person she was working with for another person.

One problem with all this sleeping around is that it creates confusion in the marketplace, giving the impression that Miss R. has true partners, when in fact she only has short-term bedfellows. Over time, people in the industry discovered R.'s pattern for what it was, and it became harder for her to find quality partners who wanted to work with her. People might still collaborate with her, but only because they needed her for a specific situation, not because they held her in the highest regard. People didn't perceive her as "partnership material," so they didn't show her loyalty or commitment.

DON'T DRIFT INTO A PARTNERSHIP

We've mentioned rushing too fast into partnerships, but there's another trap people fall into. Perhaps you've had friends who are kinda-sorta in committed relationships, but not really. These poor souls "hang out" with prospective partners, thinking that it's just casual. Because it's so casual, they never bother to ask the tough questions and to follow up with more questions when the answers they receive aren't to their liking. Then one day, these people wake up to find out that, well, they're living with someone, for heaven's sake. They're acting *as-if* they were partners, yet without the security of an actual commitment.

This happens all the time in business, and it's happened to us. For a number of years, we worked with a large organization as consultants on their conference. The organization paid us to do the legwork required to make the conference a success, relying on both our contacts and our expertise. After about a decade, the organization was having some financial trouble and was letting some of our invoices slide. One day, the organization called us up and told us that our contract wasn't being renewed.

What a shock that was. More than a shock: It was a knife to the heart. We had put all of ourselves into their events, over so many years. How could they just fire us? And emotions aside, did it even make sense for them to fire us? We had all the know-how they needed to put on the event. They couldn't do it without us. Except they could. All along, we had shared our knowledge and contacts with them. We had regarded our relationship not as a simple consulting arrangement, but as a true partnership, complete with things like loyalty and trust. But this organization no longer saw it that way. To them, we were still what we had always been—hired guns. And what do you do when money is tight and you no longer feel you need your hired guns? You don't renew their contract.

We had gotten much too cozy in this relationship. We were "living with" this organization, so to speak, yet we had never formally tied the knot. What we should have done, at a certain point, was renegotiate our relationship and formalize a legal partnership, complete with a portion of equity ownership. But at that point, we would have had to ask ourselves whether this organization really was the perfect partner for us.

No matter what kind of relationship you're currently involved in, don't allow yourself to carry on in a limbo state. Evaluate periodically what you're doing for the other party. If you're behaving like a partner, make sure you are one legally. Or if you don't want to partner, put boundaries on your responsibilities. Make a clear and determined choice for yourself to partner or not, underpinned as always by a process of discovery and careful consideration of the facts.

HAVE A PROPER DISC-USSION

Let's say you and your prospective partner are both self-aware. You know all your likes and dislikes, needs and wants, and you agree on the partnership's goals. What other questions should you ask? Returning to the questioning we offered in chapter one to help decide whether a partnership in general is right for you, we try to spend additional time fleshing out the following:

1. **What are the true motivations of a prospective partner for embarking on a venture with us?** What are their long-term goals? Do they align with ours? It's not always about the money. It might be reputational benefit, the gaining of a competitive edge, or in the case of one of our potential partners, a way out of an existing partnership.

2. **What are a prospective partner's strengths and weaknesses?** Do they complement ours? And if we combine the prospective partner's skills, competencies, and resources with ours, do we have what we need for our joint success? If not, are there ways to plug the gaps (say, by turning to an outside contractor)? Strengths are often apparent. Weaknesses are a different matter. It may be uncomfortable, but it is important to ask a potential partner what they perceive to be their weaknesses. Be blunt.

3. **What roles and responsibilities does the prospective partner wish to take on?** Again, do they complement the ones we wish to take on, or do they conflict? Do they match the prospective partner's actual skills and resources, or is it a stretch? We sometimes gravitate to what we "want" to do, rather than what we "can" or "should" do. That might not be in the partnership's best interests.

In assessing strengths and weaknesses, we've found it helpful to apply the DISC Model, based on a theory about emotions and behaviors developed by Dr. William Marston, an early 20th century psychologist.[6] Analyzing people's behaviors and personality qualities, Marston identified four basic behavioral types of normal people. His work was used to establish the DISC Assessment tool used in business to choose qualified employees based on their personality traits—each of which makes a valuable contribution to a business.[7] These four basic behavioral traits that characterize personalities are:

Dominance. D's are the dominant leaders, the people steering the bus. As entrepreneurs, they're the ones with the vision and the drive to make that vision reality. They are independent, persistent, and direct.

Influence. I's are the persuasive, inspiring, and impressive influencers. They are the salespeople of the team, promoting the vision of the D. Their focus is on the future, not the present, and on people rather than tasks.

Steadiness. Okay, S, you are the steady rudder of the ship. You keep the boat going in the right, consistent direction. D and I may zigzag all over the place, but you are the navigator, and you point the bow toward success.

Conscientiousness. As a C personality, you are the slow and critical thinker. You like having rules and processes to follow, and you follow them perfectly. Sometimes too perfectly. It's okay to be a perfectionist, but remember, this is a business, and there is nothing perfect about that.

DISC might seem like a mouthful of analytical rhetoric, but it really does help you understand what you're hearing when interviewing prospective partners, and it helps you determine if a potential partner is bringing the right skills and competencies to the table. Every business needs each letter, and it needs a proper balance between the letters. Too much D and not enough S or C, and you will create fabulous new ideas that will never be executed on a sustainable basis. In a small start-up company, you may need to be the Jack- or Jackie-of-all-trades, but very few people are good at everything. Are you going to need help to fill in a DISC letter or two? In large companies, the DISC skills get staffed in departments like Accounting, Sales, and Operations.

We knew going into our business partnership that Jim is a combo of D and I. Bob is a definite S and C, with a little D and I thrown in for good measure. Knowing this about one another, we were able to determine that we had the right combination of traits, desires, commitment, and temperament to move forward together. Alone, each of us wasn't going to achieve much. But together, we really had something. How does your prospective partner match up? Before you sign on the dotted line, throw a DISC or two at your partner. You won't regret it.

NOT A PERFECT PARTNER, BUT ONE YOU TRUST

There is one final consideration to take into account when picking a partner—a gut feeling that isn't captured in the DISC model. Do you really trust your prospective partner? Would you bet your livelihood or even your life on him or her? As romantic partners, we trust one another on a very deep, personal level, and that carried a lot of weight when we were considering forming a business relationship. We would suggest that the presence of trust can sometimes allow you to greenlight a partnership even when your and your partner's motivations, skills, and desired roles and responsibilities don't match perfectly. Trust is *that* important.

Mitchell Gold is cofounder and CEO of Mitchell Gold + Bob Williams, one of the world's leading home furnishings brands, known for their modern style sense and company ethos.[8] As Mitchell told us, "There has to be trust. I think the bottom line is, you have to be with somebody that at the very core you believe is 110 percent honest. When I met Bob (Williams), within days, I knew that he was somebody incredibly special. Then when we started talking about having a business together, I really felt (the) trust. It's hard to do that. It's hard to know that, of course, but I think that is the biggest, most gigantic thing."

FelCor is a publicly traded hotel real estate investment trust founded in 1991 by Thomas Corcoran and his partner Hervey Feldman. Perhaps you noticed—Fel is for Feldman and Cor is for Corcoran. At the time of FelCor's founding, Corcoran had known Feldman for years, having worked with him at a previous employer, the Brock Hotel Group. By 1984 Corcoran had become CEO of Brock, and he and Feldman had become good friends, even though Feldman was about a decade older. "He was my mentor," Corcoran said, "a guy I could go to as a lonely CEO with no one else to talk to, and we would, once every week, get together."

As Corcoran also recalled, the two had an enormous amount of trust in one another that served as the basis of a great partnership. They also had a shared vision for the company, as well as strongly complementary skills and aptitudes. Feldman was "more of the idea guy, certainly smarter than me, and I was the guy who was supposed to make things happen and get it done." Temperamentally, the two balanced one another out well. Feldman was more passionate and could behave irrationally at times, while Corcoran was steadier, if less imaginative. They often disagreed on issues that arose, but when they did, their mutual trust, kicked in. This allowed them to work through the disagreement in a way that brought out each of their strengths.

"We were a good yin and yang," Corcoran said. "A typical conversation would be Hervey saying, 'I think we ought to go put popcorn machines in all the lobbies,' and I'd say, 'That is a stupid fucking idea.' He'd say, 'OK.' The next day, I would go, 'You know that idea you had? Maybe it's not so stupid,' and we'd talk it through together. He had the ability to come up with some fairly significant, complicated, well-thought out plans that I at first would not usually agree with. But then I would think about it, so I always gave him credit for planting seeds that created a great partnership. He played that role in our partnership." Sadly, Feldman passed away in 2004, but FelCor lives on.

Like the two of us, Corcoran and Feldman had spent years auditioning one another for the role of business partner, maybe without even knowing it. As a result, they possessed a deep, intuitive awareness of the other's personality and capabilities. When they decided to partner, they thought through very clearly what each brought to the table, and whether they had what it took to succeed.[9]

Look around you: Is the perfect partner *for you* already present in your life? Is it your colleague, your neighbor, or a family member? Whomever you wind up choosing, make sure to get the relevant facts. Carefully analyze what your business needs and what a prospective partner might bring. Picking a business partner, like picking a spouse, should never be taken lightly. Sure, you might wind up partnering with that lovable guy who approaches you at a party with a Gucci loafer full of champagne in his hand. But only after a thousand questions have been asked and answered. And then a thousand more.

LESSONS LEARNED

* *There is no such thing as a "perfect partner." Look for the best partner for the situation you are in. Go for one you respect and can trust, one who respects and trusts you.*

* *Don't rush in. Work with your prospective partner on a short-term project and get to know him or her before you seal the deal.*

* *Identify your personal DISC profile and figure out what personality traits you need in a partner. This will help you find a partner that balances and complements you.*

* *Trust your gut when picking your partner. Do your homework, but listen to that voice inside.*

CHAPTER FOUR

DGIA
(Don't Give it Away)

One of us, Bob, jokes that he gave his life away for the sake of our partnership. When we met, Jim was a seasoned hotel guy. Hospitality wasn't just a career for him; it was his life. He thought about hotels all day, every day. Bob didn't have nearly the same kind of single-minded devotion to his work. He did interior design, sold antiques, sold real estate—a little of this, a little of that. He was experimenting in hopes of finding his true passion. Bob wished Jim would break away more from his work. He didn't like that Jim was constantly traveling and that even his spare time was taken up by talking or thinking about hotels.

By the mid-1990s, Jim was running his own one-man consulting shop, working on the side to put on a few conference events that brought together hotel industry executives. Bob, who was good at organizational and administrative tasks, helped out with tasks Jim struggled with, like using his dot matrix printer (remember, this was a long time ago), researching trends, and word processing. To Bob's mind, these conferences were truly the "third person" in their relationship, since they ate up precious down time on nights and weekends. But he had learned to put up with them.

On more than a few occasions, some well-respected hotel executives approached Jim and remarked that he was putting a lot of extra work into these conferences and not getting much in return. Why was he working for someone else? Why not create a real business around those conferences and own the events himself? Jim thought this was a pretty good idea—not just for him, but for *us*. He asked Bob what he thought about the two of us going into business together. At first, Bob was noncommittal. Although he liked the idea of seeing Jim more, he was afraid of losing himself in the vortex that was the hotel industry. He had to make sure that the arrangement was carefully tailored so that he could keep an identity of his own and not just become "Mrs. Hotel."

We began to assess what it would take for Bob to feel comfortable. Bob decided that he needed four things. First, he needed an exit plan. He was willing to devote five years of his life to jump-starting their venture, but after that he reserved the right to walk away. Second, he wanted to handle the business' creative aspects, like marketing and building the website; he was good at crunching numbers, but he didn't want to do that all day long—it just wasn't him. Third, Bob wanted to stay in the back of the house. He didn't want to be visible at the events, schmoozing people, since this was not his industry. Jim would have to handle that himself. And finally, Bob didn't want to put in Jim's crazy hours. If he was to become part of the business, he only wanted to work four days a week. He wanted time to explore his passions and outside interests.

Jim agreed to all this, and in 2000 Burba Hotel Network (BHN) was born. The rest, as they say, is history. By the five-year mark, the business was rapidly expanding, and Bob was happy with how our relationship was functioning, both inside and outside of the business. So even though he was working five days a week instead of four (poor baby, Jim says), he decided that they should continue. As of this writing, fifteen years have passed—and the business and our partnership are stronger than ever.

Bob did sacrifice his professional independence for Jim, but he didn't just give it all away. He negotiated for what he needed. We think there's an important lesson in that for anyone considering a partnership. When opportunity knocks, don't just agree to everything and anything your prospective partner requests. Understand the full value of your participation, and be sure you're getting fair value in return. Be just as cautious and circumspect when coming to terms with your new partner as you were when selecting him or her. It's a basic principle of business: Nobody will pay for something if you're willing to give it away. So don't undervalue your talents, expertise, and resources. *DGIA*.

PUT "NO" BACK INTO YOUR VOCABULARY

We wish we could say that we have always practiced DGIA in our business. Well, we almost always have. On one occasion, John, a well-known businessman in a field adjacent to ours, approached us asking if we wanted to develop a new conference together that would appeal to customers outside our core audience. It sounded great, so we plotted out a partnership together, talking through the prospective event with John in great detail. We discussed how our own company runs, our processes, the ups and downs of running a for-profit conference. We were so excited about the chance to work with John that we even hired attorneys to create an LLC for us, complete with a playbook addendum specifying exactly what each of us would do to make the event a success.

By the time we hammered out the financial elements of our business relationship, the first conference was already pretty well conceived, and John pretty well trained in the intricacies of our business. Imagine our shock when John announced that he didn't want to partner with us after all. We parted ways, and not long thereafter learned that John had launched his *own* conference business. We had given it all away—our expertise, our time, even our money in hiring attorneys—before getting a signed contract that protected our interests. There was nothing we could do about it now, other than swallow our pride and resolve never, ever to do anything like this again.

It isn't just us—many partners *do* give it away. Perhaps they lack confidence in themselves and their abilities; they fear that if they don't immediately say yes, the opportunity will vanish. Certainly our cultural programming pushes us all to say yes, and to do it quickly. We're raised to always accede to the wishes of our parents, and then when we enter business, we're told that, "the customer is always right." As consumers, we encounter marketing that urges us *not* to stop and think when deciding whether or not to sign up for a deal. Whether it's McDonald's or your local car dealer, the message is the same: "Hurry, this offer is available for a limited time only. Say yes now!"

We know many highly successful entrepreneurs, and they all confirm how easily our emotions can lead us to say "yes" when what we should be saying is "tell me again why" or "maybe" or possibly even "no." In fact, if you've been in business for a while, chances are you've given too much away on occasion. Our misadventures with John weren't the first time we gave things away. You'll recall our story in the last chapter about how we once consulted on a conference only to find that we had become a de facto partner and were doing most of the work. Our mistakes were many in that instance, but one big one was giving too much away at the outset without getting an ownership stake in return. Here again we showed our partners how to do everything, and we even put them in touch with all the right people. We didn't consider that our partners could one day potentially become our competitors—as they did. Ouch.

You simply must be willing to say "no" when negotiating a partnership. You never want to relinquish trade secrets, proprietary processes, or your contact list without receiving quite a bit in return. And as we'll discuss in more detail in chapter seven, there is something else you should never give away: Your integrity. In addition to the moral dimensions, you'll diminish your reputation in the marketplace. And once lost, your reputation is very difficult to recover.

But even when a prospective partner is asking for something that you could potentially give, you might still want to say no. It's a question of balance. When you give too much away, you wind up regretting it, and the partnership becomes laden with resentments. You can blame your partner all you want for contributing too little compared to what you think you're giving, but if you said "yes" too quickly at the outset, then it's on you.

ARRIVING AT WHAT'S FAIR

We *are* willing to say no during partnership negotiations, and we do so with some regularity. To keep ourselves grounded in the many informal partnerships we form while running our business, we do a couple of things. First, we remind ourselves of some of the primary things at stake when people form partnerships. These include:

+ Money

+ Power or control

+ Future opportunities

+ Share of ownership

+ Reputation

+ Workload responsibilities

+ Knowledge/intellectual capital

Running down this list, we tally up what we're being asked to give and compare it with what we're getting. Are the roles and rewards proportionate or equitable? Then we go on to ask ourselves a number of questions when confronted with any request from a potential partner:

1. Is giving or sharing a particular thing in our own best interests or that of the partnership?

2. Are we compromising integrity in any way by acceding to our prospective partner's request? Does it go against our beliefs or what the partnership is supposed to be all about?

3. Will acceding to a request enable our new partner to compete with us some day? Are we giving away or teaching our partner something that makes us unique?

4. If we're contemplating saying "yes" to a request, what emotion is driving us? Is it fear? What about pride? Have we given ourselves time to get past the initial jubilation of landing the new partner? Are we giving something away because we want to "please" our prospective partner? If so, is our prospective partner equally solicitous of us?

5. If we've had dealings in the past with our prospective partner, has a pattern emerged of one person giving and the other taking? Have we too often been on the giving side?

6. If we say "no" and lose the partnership, what other options are available to us?

These questions are simply guidelines designed to help spur our thinking. Even if a request from a prospective partner feels difficult or requires us to give up control, we might still say "yes," depending on the circumstances. If you're just starting out in an industry, for instance, you may have no other way of generating capital or marketing your product, so giving up a controlling share of a business might be your ticket to something bigger then you could achieve on your own. If you watch ABC's popular TV show *Shark Tank*, you can see entrepreneurs coming to this conclusion every week. They realize they need to give up more when they're just getting started, but that they'll gain a more advantageous bargaining position as they go along. If you're in this position, just make sure you're getting *something* out of the deal that makes proceeding with it worthwhile.

THE TENSION BETWEEN GIVE AND TAKE

In February 2002, our fledgling business was put to the test when we held our first big ALIS (the Americas Lodging Investment Summit) conference. The stakes couldn't have been higher. It was our first time working with the external partners we had chosen (the American Hotel and Lodging Association), and we wanted to impress them so they felt good about the new relationship. We also needed to prove to ourselves that we could work well together and achieve a success. Unfortunately, the deck was stacked against us. The events of 9/11 had happened only months before, and the country was still in shock. Businesspeople hadn't yet returned to their normal travel routines, and the economy had taken a hit. It was a difficult and awkward time to launch anything, especially an investment conference related to the travel industry. Would anyone bother to show up?

As we told each other, they had damn well better! Bob had quit his regular job to help get BHN going, and the income from Jim's full-time job was barely enough to cover our living expenses. We were watching every penny (okay, at least Bob was) and in keeping with our principle in Chapter Six, "Go All In," we had put everything we had into making the event memorable. We booked the event in Los Angeles' Kodak Theatre, a glamorous venue that had just been built to serve as the permanent home of the Academy Awards. In fact, we were the first business group to use the space. To headline the event, we hired a big name worthy of the theater, Joan Rivers. We were already over budget and couldn't afford her—Bob was freaking out. But we sucked it up and hired her anyway.

Before Joan went on, we presented what we call our ALIS Awards, given to organizations that had done the top hotel deals the past year. Each award winner received a trophy, and we had splurged for huge gold statues that looked like Academy Awards. After Joan's performance, which was bawdy and hysterical, she was sitting backstage and saw an extra one of these trophies that we hadn't given away. She picked it up and held it lovingly as if it were an Academy Award she had just received. Then she asked if she could take pictures with people as she held the award. Wow, we thought, how cool for us to get pictures of Joan with the trophy. As she got ready to leave, she turned to us and asked, "Can I take this with me?"

Bob smiled, but inside his stomach was churning. That trophy cost about $500. That might not sound like a lot today, but back then, for us, it was. Bob was planning on saving the trophy for the following year (assuming there would be a show the following year). The two of us looked at one another, and Bob whispered, "We can't give that away." But Joan was clearly so excited to have it. And she had been so kind, such a pleasure to work with. Finally Bob nodded that it was okay. Jim smiled and said warmly, "Sure, you can have it."

"Oh, thank you, thank you," Joan said, waving and pretending she was an Academy Award winner.

Bob went back to the conference office, shaking his head and saying, "Oh my God, I can't believe we gave that away." He kept saying, "Don't give it away. Don't give it away, DGIA!" And that's how we arrived at the name for this partnership principle.

We're glad we parted with that trophy—it was the right thing to do. But our tension over giving persists to this day. Jim is more inclined to give without thinking about what we're getting back, while Bob is always thinking about "what's in it for us." Jim is Mr. Yes, and Bob is Dr. No!

Which one of us is right? Neither, and both. Jim's thinking allows us to build goodwill in our industry, and what we give and do for others tends to come back to us over the long term. Bob's thinking protects us from giving away so much that we compromise our own business. In some specific instances, generosity wins out, as it did with Joan. In other cases, self-protection wins. Over the long term, it's about *knitting together* generosity and financial prudence into an overall outlook on the business. Hopefully in your partnership you'll have one party who favors generosity and another more inclined to look out for number one. If not, try to make a habit of hearing both of these voices in your own head and letting them fight it out (of course, if you start talking to yourself out loud, you've probably gone too far). Your constant back and forth on this issue will allow you to win friends in your industry while still leaving you with a healthy, viable business. Our running debate has done that for us.

ALL DGIA, ALL THE TIME

As the Joan Rivers episode suggests, the DGIA principle doesn't just apply when creating formal, legal partnerships; it applies in all kinds of situations that crop up in the course of doing business. During our first couple of years as a company, sponsors of our events, delegates, vendors, performers, and others began calling us up to ask for favors of one kind or another. Later as our business grew and we produced more and more events, we fielded many more of these requests. The individuals calling us weren't partners of ours in a legal sense, but we thought of them as partners and wanted to treat them that way. In deciding how to respond, we found ourselves running through the kinds of considerations captured in our list of questions so as to adhere to our DGIA principle.

Hotel owners, developers, or investors have often called us asking if Jim could introduce them to individuals in another city, state, or country who might be interested in doing business with them. The caller will often offer to pay a fee for this service, and we turn the fee down; as we see it, our business is connecting people and that happens all year and not just during a conference. So will Jim make the introduction? Most often, yes; it only involves a small amount of his time on the phone. When Jim says yes a little too often, Bob will step in and ask the basic question, "What's in it for us?" Jim can't just give away all of his time. Does saying "yes" to a request help us create goodwill? Will it help a customer? Does it compromise our principles or business? If the answer to the last of these questions is yes, then Jim has to set some limits. DGIA.

SWIMMING IN SUCCESS

Striking a balance between generosity and financial prudence is hard. When you don't get it right, you pay the price, sometimes for years. But when you do get it right—well, watch out, world.

Fashion designer Trina Turk had modest ambitions when she quit her job back in 1995. She wanted to create a small women's contemporary clothing collection, just enough of a business to allow her to get by while working for herself. Boy, did she succeed. As of this writing, her company Trina Turk is an iconic lifestyle brand, capturing the spirit of California in a full line of women's clothing, accessories, activewear, menswear, home fashion, footwear, and jewelry. When we sat down with Trina and hubby Jonathan Skow to ask her when her business started to take off, she told us how her first successful partnership enabled her to venture beyond womenswear into the swimwear category—but only after she had applied her version of our DGIA principle in setting up the partnership.

Trina's partner, Apparel Ventures (AV), was an established manufacturer that typically produced branded swimwear for major designers such as Ralph Lauren. AV paid the designer a royalty and produced the swimwear according to the designer's specifications. The company wanted to branch out and create its own line of swimwear that it would call "W." Attracted by Trina's trademark look emphasizing exciting prints and vivid colors, AV came to Trina and proposed a collaboration. Trina and Jonathan, a cofounder of the Trina Turk company, were flattered. Here was a manufacturer coming to *them*. How could they say no?

As excited as Trina and Jonathan were, they had the presence of mind to mull it over. In agreeing to collaborate, Trina would be contributing her unique talent and expertise to the partnership, as well as her reputation as an exciting, up-and-coming designer. What would she be getting in return? Well, a revenue stream. But was this enough? Trina and Jonathan decided that it wasn't. They wanted to continue building out the Trina Turk brand, and that meant they needed their own, branded line of swimwear. Rather than a collaboration on "W," they wondered whether AV would consider entering into a more standard licensing agreement such as it had with other designers.

It was a tough sell. Trina's brand wasn't as well established as the other brands AV produced, and it wasn't clear that Trina Turk branded swimwear would actually appeal to consumers. But Trina stood firm—she wasn't about to give away her talent and expertise if she didn't get what she felt she needed. AV finally agreed, and happily for all parties, the swimwear line took off, becoming one of the top-five swimwear brands sold at Bloomingdale's and Nordstrom. As Trina related, she couldn't have done it without AV. "Had we not partnered with a swimwear specialist, we probably wouldn't have reached the kind of volume we had. I mean, we could have made swimwear if we wanted to, but we didn't have the sales organization, the manufacturing know-how, and other components that go into making a good swimsuit." From swimwear, Trina Turk expanded into an array of other categories, becoming the lifestyle brand it is today.[10]

It's not easy to get partnerships off on the right foot. You need to be generous enough to nurture a young relationship, while mindful of the need to maintain your own integrity, reputation, and power. Prospective partners will flatter you, sometimes purposely in order to get the best possible terms. They'll play to your deepest fears and desires.

Don't give in. Don't give it away. Believe in yourself. Remember what you're all about. Trina got it right—and now she's swimming in success. You can get it right, too.

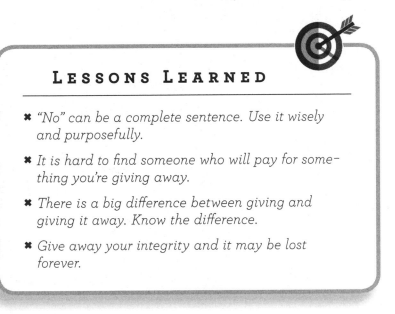

LESSONS LEARNED

* *"No" can be a complete sentence. Use it wisely and purposefully.*

* *It is hard to find someone who will pay for something you're giving away.*

* *There is a big difference between giving and giving it away. Know the difference.*

* *Give away your integrity and it may be lost forever.*

CHAPTER FIVE

Create Your Partnership Playbook

Around 2001, in the aftermath of the conflict in the Balkans, we partnered with the government of Montenegro to host an investment conference for their tourism industry. This event would be a big deal, attended by the president of Montenegro himself. To make sure we executed the event perfectly, we held a conference call every few weeks for the better part of the year with our government contacts, planning out every detail. Time zones aside, communication wasn't the easiest: we didn't speak Serbian, but fortunately our partners spoke "some" English, the word "some" often making for interesting calls. The Montenegrins were lovely to work with, but as we remember it, the answer to many questions we asked was "okay."

Can the invitation letters from the president be sent next week?

"Okay."

Was the hotel ballroom big enough to provide classroom style seating for 200?

"Okay."

Does the sun set in the West?

"Okay."

Still, we found a way to get things done, and as far as we could tell, the event would be a smashing success. On the appointed day, we traveled to the designated hotel on

Montenegro's spectacular Kotor Bay. Everything about the place seemed great. The conference room was the right size, the staff was ready in their appointed places, registration seemed to be running smoothly, and the food and drinks were all set to arrive as planned.

Then we noticed a small problem. There was only one podium on stage, not two. The entire choreography of this event was built around the use of two podiums, one on either side of the stage. We inquired where the other podium was, but nobody seemed to know anything about it (here is where speaking Serbian might have helped us). An hour went by, then another—but no second podium. We needed that extra podium for the event to appear polished and professional. The show was set to go on in only a few hours, and the minister of tourism and other dignitaries were soon to arrive.

Staff at the hotel frantically called around. It turned out the hotel had only the one podium and no podium was available at any other nearby hotel. The staff finally did manage to find a spare podium at a hotel on the other side of the country (okay, that sounds dramatic, but Montenegro isn't all that big—smaller than the State of Connecticut). The hotel sent someone to drive over, pick up the podium, and bring it back. We received it just in time.

Unfortunately, when we got it on stage, we found that the two podiums were mismatched: one was tall and slender, the other short and squat. It was not ideal (we're sticklers for detail), but we made it work, and the event proceeded as planned. Although we had almost suffered a minor heart attack, we wound up with a room full of happy Montenegrins and international investors, and that's what counted.

On our flight back to the United States, we sipped gin and tonics and thought about the podium debacle. As best as we could tell, it came down not to poor communication, but poor delegation of roles. Our contract had specified roughly what each side was to do: We were providing the content, while our partners in Montenegro were responsible for logistics. But had we talked about podiums in particular? Well, not really. We had sort of assumed they would handle that. In fact, during our many conference calls, we had never bothered to methodically run through all of our respective duties one by one. Since we had no history together, some of the details were left murky at best. In these areas, we were each left to interpret our responsibilities as *we* saw fit, leaving opportunities for miscues. It was surprising that more elements of the event hadn't gone awry.

We could have avoided the podium peccadillo—or far more serious breakdowns in our partnership—by spelling out responsibilities ahead of time. Ideally, we would have crafted what we call a "partnership playbook," an oral or written roadmap for the partnership that goes beyond the obligations laid out in a written contract. As the Ignition Consulting Group claims, "if all the partners are responsible, then none of the partners are responsible."[11] The existence of a playbook assures that not all of the partners will be responsible for a given task, but rather only the specific tasks assigned to them. The partners avoid confusion and avoid stepping on one another's toes, making it more likely that all tasks will get done with a minimum of conflict between the partners.

A partnership playbook is actually the logical extension of the process of selecting a partner. When contemplating a partnership, we research prospective partners to make sure we're compatible, but we also engage in some horse-trading, determining what each partner wants to do and what each is willing to give up. This leaves us with a rough sense of a plausible division of labor. Then, after selecting a partner, and while still finalizing the agreement, we suss out what the division of labor will *really* entail, organizing the partnership based on what has been learned so far. As we've found, specifying and divvying up the roles as tightly as possible does indeed make for much smoother sailing once operations get underway.

GET INTO THE DETAILS—
EVEN IF YOU DON'T "NEED" TO

Now, you might wonder: How deep into the details must you get? It's impossible to anticipate every little situation that might materialize in most business dealings. Trying to do so, after a point, is a thankless, tedious task. How fun is a marriage where every last item is planned out, including "sex night" from seven to eight on alternate Wednesdays? (We wouldn't know, but we imagine it's not very fun.)

The exact scope and contents of a partnership playbook will vary depending on the size of your business or partnership, the number of partners, and the abilities of each partner. As a general rule, we plan on covering the following five P's:

- ✦ Product (who will create what we're selling?)

- ✦ People (who will take care of human resources and training?)

- ✦ Promotion (who will oversee the marketing?)

- ✦ Process (who will take charge of all the fun back-end stuff like financial, billing, database management, IT, and so on?)

- ✦ Place (who will handle everything associated with the office or location?)

Within the framework of the five P's, we find ourselves spending more or less time hammering out the details depending on how familiar we are with our partner. If we know our partner well, we often don't need to do as much work up front to define roles. We're able to intuit more about what we're in for, and we've also built up more trust. If things go askew, we can take comfort in knowing that each party will pitch in to get the job done. On the other hand, if we have only recently met our partner, and we don't have time to indulge in a prolonged "dating" period, then crafting a highly detailed partnership playbook is itself an opportunity to get to know one another better. We might not perform every last task as specified in the playbook, but we'll have the structure we need to make a strong initial go of it.

When our colleague Tom Corcoran and his partner Hervey Feldman set up FelCor, a company that owns and operates hotels, they agreed that Tom would handle the operational side of the business and Hervey would serve as the creative "brains" of the enterprise. As Tom told us, "Hervey admitted that he hated doing what he called "nit-shit." He hated doing that part of it, but he was what I'd call a great idea man and a great thinker, and he had an amazing ability to come up with extremely bright, intelligent, complicated deals that would blow me away."[12]

The two didn't have to spell out every last detail, since they had known one another well for years and shared a mutual trust and respect. Even so, Tom remembers they "did have a fairly specific discussion" establishing some of the tasks that he would handle, such as payroll, managing the office, and personnel matters. Hervey, therefore, would play the lead role in negotiating deals, "and then, once we had agreed on a deal, I would make it all happen." Beyond that, the two "felt out" a lot of the specific roles and responsibilities. A bit more fluidity in the arrangement worked for them because their talents and skills were so strikingly different.

Bertram van Munster and Elise Doganieri had a much different conversation when they founded their production

company, World Race Productions. Long-term romantic partners who joined together to create the ten-time Emmy award-
winning television show *The Amazing Race*, they possessed
knowledge and experience in each of their industries; Bertram was a television producer, and Elise was in advertising.
From the beginning, the two decided that although they would
co-own the business and share credit as co-creators of the
show, Bertram would take the lead but would always consult
with Elise on final decisions.

Elise, meanwhile, would develop her television chops by
taking on a variety of roles—field producer, producer, supervis-
ing producer, executive producer—that would allow her to learn
the business from the ground up. What made this unusual partnership situation work, Elise told us, was the mutual respect
the two shared, as well as the function each partner always
served as a valued sounding board for the other. Bertram valued her opinion, and Elise felt free to share it openly. "The big
benefit that we have together is that we're not going to sugar
coat anything. We're going to be sometimes painfully, bru-
tally honest, but you know you're going to get the truth, and
you're going to hear it from somebody who has both of your
best interests in mind."[13]

Like Tom/Hervey and Bertram/Elise, the two of us had
built a strong personal relationship for years before going
into business together. We each knew roughly how our business roles would break down. Beyond this, we felt comfortable leaving quite a bit of our playbook unwritten, so much so
that as our business got underway, we found ourselves making some surprising adjustments. As a former partner in an
accounting firm, Jim would have normally insisted that *he*
oversee accounting and finance. Yet given the roles assigned
to him as our company's public face, he just didn't have time to
monitor transactions with literally hundreds of vendors, event

sponsors, and other partners. So Bob took over accounting. As Jim quickly learned, Bob was even more fastidious than he would have been, balancing the books to the very last penny. Realizing that Bob could handle the job, he felt comfortable relinquishing control for the sake of achieving a proper balance in the partnership.

Even if you already know one another well, it's probably worth spending more time than we did assigning roles. Prompting a discussion about roles and responsibilities makes sense for any number of reasons. First, it can help you confirm how serious your future partner really is. If your partner shies away from talking about the "small stuff," that could be a sign of trouble—your partner may only be "dating" you and may not be ready to tie the knot. Second, a conversation about roles and responsibilities affords you a good opportunity to review and refine your business plan. When you examine your operations methodically, you might uncover parts of the business you hadn't thought about.

Third, if you find yourselves readily agreeing about who will take what specific task, that's great—it can be a short conversation—but perhaps you don't know one another as well as you think. If you find yourselves butting heads, each of you clamoring to oversee the same part of the business, then that might be a warning sign, too: At this stage, you shouldn't be disagreeing all that much over what each of you will do.

If it turns out you both want to handle certain tasks, then you'll have to negotiate over who does it. One person needs to bear primary responsibility; if both people are assigned to a task, quite often *neither* of them will do it, and the task doesn't get done. On the other hand, if you find that neither of you wants to handle a given task, then you'll have to figure out a way to outsource it. Either way, at least you'll have a clearer picture of how your operations will work, and you'll be able to resolve potential conflicts early, before they have a chance to bog down your business.

A ROADMAP FOR THE FUTURE

Creating a playbook has yet another benefit: It can help long-time partners by setting them up for *future* changes to the business. When we signed on as a partner in our Asia Pacific investment conference, we had already served for several years as a consultant to the event, so we knew our two Hong Kong partners well. That didn't matter—we prompted everyone to discuss in detail our respective roles and responsibilities. And we didn't just discuss them: We formalized the partnership playbook on a three-column spreadsheet, enumerating dozens of tasks, assigning responsibility for each to either ourselves or our partners, and specifying who was going to contribute in a supportive role to the task.

Once we had the spreadsheet set up, we gave it more thought and reconvened on a couple of occasions to review and revise it. We wound up reallocating roles depending on the partners' interest or bandwidth. In a couple of instances, we found that the words on paper didn't clearly communicate the task needing to be executed as well as we thought, so we more carefully delineated what each of us was going to do. Program content development and speaker identification tasks went to the partner who actually lived and worked in Asia because he was most familiar with the hotel dealmakers there. Since Bob was fastidious in his handling of money, we took on the accounting role. The third partner in our group was most interested in marketing and promotion, so she focused her attention on those tasks. All of this extra planning served us well, helping us transition seamlessly into a pre-existing partnership. We could each execute our responsibilities without tripping over one another.

Years later, as our business grew and we added new events in Japan and Singapore, we returned to that same spreadsheet to divvy up the new executional responsibilities that would be required. Programming, again, went to our partner in Asia and his colleagues in Tokyo. Everything else, however, was more evenly split between us and our third partner. While we remained the prime organizer of the Hong Kong event, our third partner took over much of the logistics of the Japan and Singapore events. If we hadn't had an existing partnership playbook, launching in these new countries might have occasioned conflict and confusion. But because we had it, the execution was much less stressful.

In some cases, partnerships do so well that outsiders want to invest in them or acquire them outright. Here, too, a playbook can prove immensely useful. Why? Well, the better defined your operations are, the easier they are to explain to an outsider. A potential buyer will always want to know what he or she is getting. A legal partnership agreement conveys some of that, but buyers want to know *exactly* who is doing what in the business, and what that would look like once the business has been acquired. With a partnership playbook, you don't have to give a vague answer. You can open your notebook or click on your spreadsheet and all the roles and responsibilities are right there in writing. Particularly when there are multiple partners, prospective suitors are cautious and inquisitive about what each partner brings to the table.

At the very least, everyone—even longtime partners—should create a partnership playbook simply as a way of hedging against risk. A podium peccadillo or two is no big deal, but we've suffered through some fairly uncomfortable situations due to our failure to nail down roles and responsibilities with our own vendors, clients, and colleagues. In the case of one event we helped create during the early years of our business, it turned out that we really didn't know our partners that well. They were supposed to handle marketing, accounting and delegate registration, and we would handle sponsor sales and provide the event's content. We assumed that our partners had significant resources that they could put behind their duties. They were a big organization, or so we thought.

If we had created a playbook and gone methodically through the roles that make up "marketing," it would have become apparent at the outset that their "marketing team" consisted of one freelancer, and that they weren't equipped to handle registration tasks for an event the size of the one we were planning. Instead, we discovered these things in real time, when faced with tasks in urgent need of completion. Confusion ensued, and we were forced to take over the marketing and outsource registration, adding expense and stress. If our near heart attack in Montenegro didn't cause us to mend our ways, this situation sure did. Since then, we've always insisted on creating a playbook when embarking on partnerships.

A partnership playbook is an often neglected part of due diligence. When people start dating and fall in love, they tend to brush off the details and say to one another, "Let's worry about it later. We'll be fine. We'll figure it out as we go along." But "later" comes up faster than you think. And all too often, you're *not* fine. Take our advice, get to know one another, up close and personal. Talk about the small stuff now.

GETTING THE PLAYBOOK RIGHT

Although partnership playbooks are fairly straightforward, there are some finer points to consider when crafting one. First, **be alert to the play of ego**. Most successful people like to be "in charge" even when they're not suited for a given role. The CEO title sounds glamorous, but are you *really* prepared to meet with investors, talk to the media, set strategy, and do all the other myriad things a good CEO does? Do you even *want* to? Be honest about your own limitations. If you can't swim, stay out of the deep end. If you can't carry a tune, don't sing in the choir. It's better to be honest with your partner than to let him or her down.

Make sure others are honest, too. For every area of the business, determine who wants to be in charge, but also ask if that person *should* be in charge. Consider factors like past experience, whether people inside and outside the business will accept that person handling the tasks in question, and whether that person is really committed to the role. Talk frankly about motivation and whether ego is playing a role in how the tasks are being divided.

Second, **create some kind of mechanism for updating the playbook**. Markets change, and so do people. Your partner who ten years ago signed up to handle all of back-end operations when she was single and had nothing else to do in her free time might not want all that responsibility now that she is married with two kids. Or she might simply be tired of operations and feel ready to take on more responsibility in a CEO role. Having a mechanism in place to update the playbook helps you anticipate changing needs and desires and head off any problems before they arise. You can also adjust for changes in the business, adding or reducing responsibilities and bringing in new partners as the situation demands. We hold conversations about our partnership playbooks every two to three years, but if your business or industry is undergoing rapid change, you might wish to do it even more frequently.

Third, **don't overplay the playbook**. On one occasion, Jim found himself endlessly revising the playbook-like addendum to a formal partnership agreement our attorney drafted for us. Jim kept loading in more and more clauses specifying what each party would do and when. The document got longer and longer, our attorney Rick more and more frustrated. Finally Rick pulled Jim aside. "Look, man, it's a piece of paper. If your partnership is going to succeed or fail, it won't be because of this document."

Jim wasn't creating an actual playbook; he was making the mistake of conflating the playbook with a *legal agreement*, and the deeper mistake of taking the definition of roles too far. As useful as a playbook is in preventing potential snafus down the road, it won't solve underlying problems in any partnership. A playbook is no substitute for trust, respect, or for picking the right partner in the first place. If you find yourself defining roles obsessively, ask yourself why that is: Are you nervous the partnership won't work? If so, why is that? Maybe your gut is telling you that you have the wrong partner, or that you've rushed too quickly into the partnership, or that your partner isn't as committed as he or she claims. On the other hand, maybe it's *you* who isn't ready to partner. Whatever the case, overplaying the playbook is a sign that something isn't right. Pay attention.

A fourth and final guideline: **Have fun**. Although "roles and responsibilities" sounds pretty serious, the discussion can be as relaxed and enjoyable as you want it to be. In 2014 the team of the first movie we co-produced, *Space Station 76,* expressed interest in partnering with us on a reality TV show idea we had. We won't bore you with the details . . . well, okay, since you asked—Bob happens to be a member of the Scottish Clan "Hay," and the show takes place at a castle in Scotland that is run as an historical attraction and holiday rental place. Guests can stay in centuries old rooms, see where Mary Queen of Scots slept in the 16th century, and dine in the "tenth Best Tea Room in Scotland." Castle stones and home-baked scones. Whisky trails and ghostly tales.

In any case, we evaluated closely whether this team would be a good partner for us on our show idea, and we decided they would be. Having worked with them on the film, we had come to respect their work ethic, strengths, and storytelling abilities. After several long telephone calls, we came to an agreement on our vision for the show. It was then time to create the playbook. We could have done another phone call, but we thought, *I don't think so. Let's meet face-to-face and do this over a few rounds of good Scottish whisky* (Reader's note: In Scotland, it's spelled "whisky," in the US it's "whiskey").

We met in a Scottish-themed bar in downtown Los Angeles. Lots of tartan plaid. Stuffed deer heads on the walls. Bagpipe music in the background. We sat together for hours, talking about all the logistics the producers would take care of, including equipment, actors, sound technicians, and so on. We talked about our role, too, which in this case turned out to be financial as well as "the talent." Of course, we were contributing the story itself, which involved two Americans heading to Scotland to find their heritage and getting into some hilarious situations at the castle because of their zealous desire to "improve" things the American way. Round after round of whisky was served. Laughs were shared by all. We came away a little buzzed, jazzed about the project we were about to embark on, and confirmed in our thinking that this partnership was the *right* one. Our playbook was in place. As of this writing, we've completed the teaser reel for the show and are waiting to see if the idea gets picked up by a network. Keep your fingers crossed!

YOU NEVER GET A SECOND CHANCE AT A FIRST TIME (WELL, ALMOST NEVER)

When we first got together as a romantic couple, we became involved in the Human Rights Campaign (HRC), a national LGBT lobbying organization. We weren't necessarily gay rights activists, but we felt strongly that our local community—California's Orange County—needed to "wake up" from its conservative haze on the issues. At this time in the early 1990s, marriage equality was a distant dream, and LGBT rights were few and far between. A number of HRC supporters decided to partner on an event in order to raise money for the organization. The two of us agreed to serve on a committee that would plan and execute an HRC summer "garden party" in Newport Beach, the first of its kind on the West Coast.

Since we both have "lead, not follow" personalities, we weren't quite sure how serving on a committee we didn't chair would work out. But we thought it would be a good way to spend time together (not knowing that in a few years we would spend 24/7 together) while contributing to a cause we felt strongly about.

As the planning process got underway, our intimate garden party turned into "Hollywood Comes to Orange County." A couple of our "partners" on the committee with Hollywood connections went a bit wild, inviting celebs like Broadway's original Dream Girl Sheryl Lee Ralph to attend. The stakes were getting higher by the minute, but unfortunately no clear direction existed as to who was doing what, when, and how. Partnership playbook? You've got to be kidding! The two of us were working on promotional pieces for the event, coercing friends of ours to design mailing pieces. It turned out that someone else on the committee had already designed a mailer and had it printed.

Likewise, we had worked our connections at the host hotel to get a "deal," only to find out that one of our committee partners had also been negotiating with another hotel staffer on another deal. So much wasted time and energy, and meanwhile, other important parts of the planning weren't getting done. The temperature on the day of the event was supposed to be in the triple digits, but nobody had made any special preparations to keep the celebrities and other partygoers cool. The garden party appeared headed for disaster, and committee members were arguing and lashing out at each other like mothers-in-law in a boxing ring.

Happily, the party turned out to be a success, despite our hapless coordination. The celebs arrived, the temperature only reached 90, the hotel found a few umbrellas they would let us use for free, a sellout crowd attended, and the party made some money for HRC. As the party was wrapping up, our fellow committee members made a fast exit with most of the guests. We stayed behind to gather up unsold silent auction items that committee members had just left on the tables. We never saw some of those committee members, our partners, again.

As we finally started to make our way out of the hotel an hour after the party ended, we came upon two of the celebs sitting at a table in the lobby bar. We were exhausted, sweating, bitching, and probably looked like we needed "the cocktail cure." The celebs invited us to join them for a drink. For the next hour, we had the most delightful conversation with Academy Award® nominee Michael Jeter and newly minted gay activist Candace Gingrich, who had just made one of her first speeches as an HRC spokesperson. The conversation bounced back and forth between HRC, boyfriends, girlfriends, Michael's new film role, Candace's relationship with her brother Newt (who was Speaker of the House of Representatives at the time), and, of course, the heat. What a fun way to end a pretty miserable committee experience. A good partnership playbook for this event would have made the event much more pleasant for us, and no doubt a much more successful fundraiser for HRC.

Because of this experience, we resisted getting more involved in committee work for some time. Several years later, a good friend, Mr. Rick, talked us into hosting the "second first annual" HRC garden party in Orange County at our house in Laguna Beach. As hosts, *we* got to help organize the committee.

And organize we did. We met regularly at our house, with all members of the committee required to attend. We fed them and gave them drinks (food and booze work great when you're trying to get people to do something). Putting in place our partnership playbook principle, we structured the committee so that the relationships, roles, and responsibilities were better defined, the players qualified, and the motivations aligned. Each committee member worked on areas of the event where he or she felt best suited. We identified overlapping and coordinated tasks. No one felt left out, and no one felt overburdened. As the head honcho, Mr. Rick kept everyone on point.

The result? The Washington DC headquarters of HRC heard about our upcoming garden party, the hundreds of ticket sales, and the money coming in. The HRC president at the time, Elizabeth Birch, brought the entire HRC network of area leaders to Orange County to attend the event and hold their national meetings. Our second first annual garden party was a huge success, and it jump-started the HRC Orange County organization, which soon became the fastest growing chapter in the United States. Our garden party became a model for how HRC committee members and "partners" working together could create something powerful for the organization.

Business partnerships, personal relationships, and in fact most things in life hinge on solid execution. To execute well, you need to know your roles. Garden parties aside, you usually don't get a second chance to get off to a good start. If you untangle the brambles of execution *before* you sign on the dotted line, you increase the odds that your partnership will flourish and grow.

LESSONS LEARNED

* *A partnership playbook spells out the who, what, when, where, how, and why of the partnership. It's essential for a smoothly running business and partnership.*

* *In your playbook, figure out who is handling the five Ps: product, people, process, promotion, place.*

* *While the playbook is essential, don't overplay it. It won't cure all ills, and it's no substitute for a weak partnership.*

* *Periodically review and revise the playbook as needed to keep the partnership current and running smoothly.*

CHAPTER SIX

Go All In

When our colleague Tom Corcoran co-founded FelCor Lodging Trust back in 1991, he thought he knew his partner Hervey Feldman pretty well. The two had worked together and been friends for years. Yet Corcoran was in for a big surprise. Four to five years into their partnership, with the business thriving, Feldman suddenly became depressed. Not just a little depressed—*severely* depressed. He became "basically incapable of communicating," Corcoran told us, and unable to work.

Months passed, and Feldman wasn't getting any better. He revealed to Corcoran that he had long suffered from a serious mental illness, a bipolar disorder. He had known about it for years and hidden it from the world; only his family knew. Corcoran was shocked. Feldman had always behaved a little erratically; he missed meetings and made outlandish statements that seemed to come out of nowhere, yet he was so brilliant that Corcoran and others around Feldman had always written it off as the charming idiosyncrasies of a creative genius.

If Corcoran had known Feldman's diagnosis at the outset, he would have not risked his steady paycheck to start a business with him. Now that they were partners, he faced a critical choice: Bail out of the partnership, or stand by his friend and find a way to carry on with the business. Many people might have chosen to bail, but Corcoran opted not to. Instead he took on more responsibility for the business. He "cleaned up the mess," so to speak, on occasions—and there were many—when Feldman's erratic behavior threatened to get out of hand, and he protected Feldman by hiding his condition from the outside world. After eighteen months, Feldman recovered from his depression and was able to resume normal activities. By 1998, however, he relapsed and again largely detached himself from the company, this time for a period of three years. By the early 2000s, he was phasing himself back in again when he became sick with cancer. He passed away in 2004 at the age of sixty-seven.

We had no idea about any of this until an interview we did with Corcoran. We were saddened to learn of Feldman's struggles but deeply impressed with Corcoran's unwavering commitment. Corcoran had never even entertained the possibility of abandoning Feldman. Of the extra work he had to take on, he remarked, "I just did it. And I think Hervey would have done the same for me if the shoe had been on the other foot." In Corcoran's mind, he hadn't just signed a legal document when forming the partnership; he'd made a personal and emotional pledge to Hervey. "We had made a deal, and I was going to honor it. I guess I always felt that I wouldn't have been as successful as I was but for Hervey, and so that was worth my loyalty to him. I felt very lucky and fortunate, because FelCor would not exist without the Fel."[14]

Many partners retreat when the going gets tough. Sometimes they check out emotionally and behave more passively. Other times they bow out by selling their stake. The adversities that drag down these partnerships are often far less extreme than mental illness. Maybe sales are slower than anticipated. Or the work is less fun. Or goals, priorities, or life circumstances have changed. Or conflict has arisen between the partners. No matter how much effort you put in up front to vet partners, negotiate a basic framework for the partnership, and flesh out roles and responsibilities, you can't predict the future. When the going gets tough, will you be prepared to stick it out? Or will you be quick to hit the road?

If you want your partnership to succeed, you *must* commit wholeheartedly at the outset, just as Corcoran did. Go all in and proclaim your intention to persevere, even if obstacles arise. As your partnership gets off the ground, *make good on your commitment*. Keeping promises is easy during the early, honeymoon days. The challenge comes later, when things aren't so new, exciting and fresh, and when your partner's less attractive sides become apparent. If each partner is all in, all the time, the partnership stands a much better chance of weathering the inevitable storms. And if you do go down together, you will at least know you did all you could to be a great partner.

THERE'S NO ACCOUNTING FOR WEAK COMMITMENT

The two of us have seen firsthand how vulnerable an organization can become when key partners are less than fully committed. Earlier in his career, Jim was a partner in a midsize accounting firm that served clients in the hospitality industry. The firm was growing rapidly, expanding from fifteen offices to more than thirty over a six- to eight-year period. This expansion largely took place as the firm acquired smaller accounting firms so as to keep pace with competitors, who were also aggressively filling out their footprints.

As new offices joined the firm's network, a lot of happy talk circulated around the firm. New partners were "thrilled to be joining the partnership" and looked forward to many successful years. They were willing to work hard and help make the firm succeed. It all sounded so wonderful. Except it wasn't. A recession hit, dealing a heavy blow to hospitality clients. The firm's major competitor went out of business, and Jim's firm was in financial trouble as well. Its bankers were clamping down on receivables, putting restrictions on spending. At this critical juncture, everybody had to pull together and sacrifice for the good of the business. Unfortunately, many of the partners in the recently acquired offices had no interest in doing that. Instead they tried to exercise escape clauses in their contracts. Jim's firm wound up shrinking just as rapidly as it had grown. Beset by the cost of settling contract disputes, eventually, it, too, went out of business.

The unraveling of his firm made a huge impression on Jim. This organization was well established, with a history dating back a century. If everyone had pulled together, the firm might have made it. Personnel in the core fifteen offices were extremely loyal, and they were willing to work harder and take pay cuts to carry the firm through to better times. The new guys just didn't see it that way. They had agreed to partner, but they hadn't gone all in yet.

PARTNERING BEYOND THE PLAYBOOK

We're not saying you should remain on a sinking ship as a noble testament to your undying loyalty. If you're about to sustain serious losses or irreparable damage to your integrity or reputation, you clearly need to get out for the sake of your own survival, and the escape clauses in many partnership agreements reflect that reality. The question is how early and easily you exercise those escape clauses, and more generally, how intent you are on contributing to the partnership from the outset. Partners who are "all in" stick with the partnership even when it's tempting to leave or step back. They buck up and demonstrate grit for the sake of the common good, and they're not scared off by the first sign of bad news. They feel a responsibility to do whatever they can, within reason, to help the partnership succeed.

The emotional commitment that "all in" partners feel leads them to go beyond the strict letter of what their contract may require, and even beyond what their partnership playbooks might envision. A contract might specify a dozen actions a partner must perform to satisfy the legal requirements; a partnership playbook might translate those dozen actions into a few dozen more specific tasks. But you can't define *everything* that might be required in a real-life situation. Grey areas will exist, and in the heat of the moment, when the business hangs in the balance, a partner who is "all in" will step up anyway and do what must be done to help the business win. Partnership for a person who is "all in" isn't *ever* about a formal document. It's about a spirited desire to give of oneself for the sake of the common good.

As important as a partnership playbook is, it's still just a guideline for action. Tom Corcoran didn't consult his playbook when picking up the slack for Hervey Feldman. He did so because he could and because his heart was in the right place. Partnerships between committed parties operate on a higher level than other arrangements. In these partnerships, the parties consistently look for opportunities to give of themselves. They're asking, "What can I do that will push the partnership forward," trusting that their partners are also asking the same question. And guess what? They usually are.

PICK A COMMITTED PARTNER

Our discussion thus far suggests another question we ask when selecting a partner. Is our prospective partner really ready to make an "all-in" commitment? Is she as intent on the partnership succeeding as we are? And does she have the time and energy to commit? Going all in doesn't require you to spend all your time on a partnership; many people in business are engaged with a number of partnerships at once. But it does require that you allot sufficient time to make your partnership all it can be, and that you make a focused effort during that time to execute on your responsibilities. Does your prospective partner get this? Is she capable of pulling her weight and executing reliably, on occasion even going above and beyond what the playbook requires?

Answering these questions is trickier than it might seem. Parties to a partnership might think of themselves as fully committed and yet wind up disappointing you. That's because parties can reasonably diverge in how they define "strong commitment." In one of our very first partnerships, we had a great idea for an event, and we engaged a much larger organization to partner with us on it. We had a signed deal and were thrilled to get going. Because this event was critical to our financial future, we were more than 100 percent invested in its success. We thought our partner was, too. We scheduled a conference call to kick off our collaboration and talk through our initial steps in more detail. As the call got underway, we raised the question of what we would charge people to attend the event. A person on our partner's side who handled financial questions— we'll call him Ted—hadn't showed up. "Where's Ted?" we asked. "Why isn't he on the call?"

"Oh," one of this colleagues responded, "He's the CFO. He doesn't have time to be on a conference call. I'll just take notes and give them to him, and he can look over the notes."

To us, this response signaled that our partner wasn't fully engaged with us. In truth, that wasn't the case. We were only a three-person shop at the time, so going "all in" meant having us all there on the call. We shouldn't have expected that all of the most senior people at our partner organization would participate in the call. From their point of view, that wasn't necessary or appropriate. Even without their CFO present, this large, hierarchical organization was in fact devoting suitable resources, and our subsequent success bore that out. Full commitment can mean very different things to large and small organizations, so you must tailor expectations accordingly.

Misunderstandings can also arise about the extent of a partner's commitment when you're operating across a cultural divide. Some years ago, we entered into a venture with a partner in Japan to produce a hotel investment conference there. Everything looked great: We knew the partner fairly well, felt comfortable with our relationships, and set up a clear, workable partnership playbook. Our job was to provide the backbone and infrastructure of the event (i.e. determine the shape, marketing, accounting, vendor coordination, pricing, and ideas for content). Since we had limited contacts in that country and little knowledge of the culture, our partner was supposed to work the scene and bring on large companies as sponsors to help pay for the event and locate the right speakers.

Unfortunately, interest in the local market was low. Very low. This puzzled us; the market was one of the biggest in the world for hotels, and by all rights our event there should have been a rousing success. Our frustration mounted because it seemed that our partner wasn't doing much to generate demand. In other markets we were in, we had a simple formula. You picked up the phone, called the right people, generated interest in the event, and nailed down sponsorship commitments. In this case, we pushed and prodded our partner to do more, to no avail. He struggled to make the calls, and when he did, nothing ever came of them. After three years, three events and a great deal of effort, our event was still losing money. We had no choice but to shut it down. We'd put 100 percent of our effort in at our end, but it appeared that we'd chosen a partner who was far less engaged. What a disappointment!

As we thought more about this failure, however, we realized that our partner might not have been as uncommitted as we'd thought: Perhaps he had been making an effort, but his understanding of what he needed to do had simply been different than ours. We learned that in his culture, you didn't just pick up the phone and make a sales call. That was considered uncouth, and it got you nowhere. Instead, you nurtured long-term relationships that eventually turned into concrete sales opportunities. You took a prospect to lunch three, five, even ten times over a period of months or years before having anything to show for it. Once you got a sale, however, you could count on years of loyalty. Our expectations of our partner had been totally unrealistic, and more than that, our entire business model for the event had probably been unworkable. Our partner had been trying to do his part, in a way that made sense to him. By pushing him to make more calls, we were only frustrating him, trying to fit him into a foreign paradigm that wouldn't work.

Our former partner has since come back to us wondering what it would take for us to agree to try to put the event on again. Conditions in the local market have changed, and our partner now thinks the event will get more traction. Also, he has been working hard all along to develop relationships, and as a result is in a position to do some deals. In fact, he already has one large company on board as a sponsor as well as a clear strategy for bringing on other big sponsors. As of this writing, we've pledged our willingness to partner again, assuming our partner can meet certain conditions. We're willing to try again because we realize that his intentions were good—he really did want to see our venture succeed. Culture and different perspectives can get in the way and cause discord, but if you're willing to be patient, good will and an intention to make a partnership work can win out in the end.

COMMIT TO BEING COMMITTED

This experience led us to an important lesson: When we are confronted by a partner who seems far less engaged than we had hoped or than we are, we try not to take it personally and rush to judgment. Rather, putting our emotions aside, we probe what might be going on. Do we have different expectations about what it means to be "all in"? Has our partner experienced a setback that is preventing him from engaging as fully as he might like? Have his interests changed, or does he now shoulder more commitments than before? If so, is there anything we can do—say, restructuring the partnership, dividing up duties differently, or adopting a different process—that might allow our partner to do his share?

We also try to ask ourselves if we're really engaged appropriately. Are we putting as much into the partnership as we think we are? Perhaps our partner is simply responding to perceived lack of enthusiasm or effort on *our* part. Looking back at the collapse of Jim's former accounting firm, it seems pretty clear that the new partners who bailed at the first sign of misfortune weren't the only parties who hadn't gone all in. The existing partners at Jim's firm hadn't, either. In signing on the new partners, they probably hadn't devoted enough care, attention, and resources to welcoming them in and forging a common culture. No surprise that the new partners didn't feel much loyalty. Loyalty and respect aren't just given. They're *earned*.

A partner might also be pulling back because they perceive you're *too* engaged in the partnership. Over the years, we've sometimes committed the sin of putting in too much and micromanaging the partnership. This can irritate partners and cause them to draw back. They think: "Why should I bother to engage if they're going to do all the work? They obviously don't need me or care what I think." As they carry less of the burden, we wind up doing even more, sacrificing ourselves for the good of the business. Of course, we wind up resenting the perceived imbalance of effort, even though we're the ones whose actions invited our partners to pull back. We fix these situations by reining in our exuberance and giving our partners more opportunity to contribute. More often than not, what we took as signs of disinterest wither away, and our partners are able to make the project their own. We feel better because we have a sense that we really are "in this together." Problem solved.

It's often not easy to hang in there with a partner who isn't pulling his weight. In the past, we struggled with a partner who didn't seem to be driving very hard to make our venture a success. We had to push to get him to take even the smallest of actions. It frustrated us. We didn't suspect anything nefarious was going on; our partner had probably just over-committed himself on other initiatives, and our venture isn't top on his priority list. Discovering that he is very comfortable operating like the college student who waits to the last minute then crams all-night for the final exam, we created more formal (and padded) deadlines for us all to make sure that things get done. Living so close to the "edge" like this may make the venture less successful, but we hung in there and made it work. The venture didn't fail, but neither was it as successful or as fun as we had imagined. Still, we continued to believe in our partner. We didn't enter the partnership lightly, and we won't exit it lightly. We're committed to being committed.

BABUSHKAS, VODKA, AND THE
MAKING OF A LASTING PARTNERSHIP

We've said it before: Don't rush into a partnership. Now you understand a bit better why. More than just researching your prospective partner, thinking through the pros and cons, assessing your compatibility, negotiating the relationship, and hashing out a playbook, we think it's best to allow for an extended trial period, especially when you're dealing with your most important partnerships. Spend as much time as possible getting to know and possibly working with your partner before you make the relationship permanent and go all in. Allow time for the decision to commit to come to you naturally. It's fun to fall head over in heels in love with someone, but the deeper, quieter, more abiding love that sustains a successful, long-term relationship requires time to take hold. You sometimes don't even know it's growing and deepening—and then one day you do know. When this day comes, you can finally go "all in" with confidence. Your partnership is the real deal. And you've earned it.

In the case of our personal relationship, each of us didn't know immediately that we would spend the rest of our lives with the other. We thought our relationship held promise during the initial months of dating, but we didn't *know*. So after a year of dating, we decided to test our suspicions out by moving in together. Our relationship continued to thrive, but even after a year or so of this, we still weren't ready to go all in. Well, one of us wasn't ready. Jim knew fairly early on that Bob was "the one," and he believed he was ready to commit for life. Bob, however, was much more cautious, preferring to wait before committing.

Bob had been on his own for years, tormented by an unhappy family situation. Since coming out during his late twenties, he had worked hard to build up his own identity as an independent gay man, and he feared letting another man in, even Jim, whom he loved. His reluctance to go all in was reflected some- what humorously in his attitude about his clothes. Jim wanted to store all of our clothes together in the same closet, since in his mind that was what couples did. Bob resisted; he wanted a separate closet for his clothes, and he even wanted to label his clothes with his name, so that we would know whose were whose when they came back from the dry cleaners. *Oy vey* . . .

Happily, this all changed after a two-week trip we took together in 1991 to the former Soviet Union, just a few months before the fall of the communist regime. Jim had to go to St. Petersburg (then known as Leningrad) as a consultant to the city government, and he was bringing his father Ed and sis- ter Jeanne along as "official tourists" to get a feel for the city and what it might offer travelers. He invited Bob to come along as well. Although Bob was a big fan of all things Russian, he hesitated to say "yes." Was Bob ready to spend so much time with the family? Maybe a little too much togetherness? This was getting serious! On the other hand, he didn't want to forego a once-in-a-lifetime chance to visit Russia. Also, he had declined a previous invitation to take a trip with Jim's family, and it had hurt Jim's feelings. Bob didn't want to do that again. It was time for him to take a risk.

The trip turned out to be every bit as memorable as we had dreamed—and then some. Although homophobia in the USSR prevented the two of us from behaving openly like boyfriends, we were able to overlook this and immerse ourselves in the cul- ture and our surroundings. We didn't think too much about the listening devices we were told would be in our room, the KGB agents we knew were watching us, or the random searches of our luggage we were told to expect. We knew we had to be on this trip as "business colleagues." Between the grimness of everyday life behind the iron curtain, the glorious Russian architecture and historical sites, and the endless stream of vodka shots, the experience was surreal from beginning to end. Sharing the adventure also took our relationship to a new level. As the days ticked by, Bob found that he liked Jim's father and sister, and he was coming to bond with them. The emotional walls Bob had put up were starting to crumble, just as the walls holding together the Soviet Union soon would.

The single greatest bonding experience between the two of us and between Bob and Jim's family took place one cold, snowy day. We made a harrowing three-hour drive from Leningrad through a blizzard, sitting next to a twenty-gallon open tub of gas in the back end of the Soviet version of a Volkswagen van, with a chain smoking driver (did we mention gas fumes?) grumbling in Russian about how this was insane. Having survived that, our party and the KGB agents/guides arrived in the picturesque and ancient city of Novgorod. With no time to rest or recuperate, we were whisked away to "lunch" at a neighborhood "restaurant" to see how the locals really live.

Enter four Americans into a crowded, hole-in-the-wall, smoke-filled tavern. We were escorted to a banquet style table, on which rested three vodka bottles. We should mention that the vodka was not our usual Belvedere or Grey Goose brands, but rather some type of locally fermented potato liquid that was put into a bottle labeled "vodka." Soon, we were joined by several non-English speaking comrades who smiled politely and then proceeded to pour the vodka into shot glasses placed in front of each of us. The toasts began, one after the other. With each toast it was down the hatch with this Russian firewater. Each person at the table had to give a toast until we made our way back around to the end of the table. We were told by the KGB guides that it was an insult not to down the shot of vodka, so we all did our best to preserve the Soviet/American partnership taking root at the banquet table.

Somewhere during the toasting, maybe after the fifth or sixth, Ed rose from the table and wandered over to another table close by, where a group of babushka types (that's Russian for grandma) were doing their own version of the vodka toasts. They were speaking a dialect similar to a Polish/Russian mix that only Jim's Polish dad could understand. Before we could say *nostrovia* (Russian for "cheers") for the seventh time—or was it eighth?—Ed was dancing around the babushka table with a Russian grandma.

We laughed, toasted some more, and finally ate—chicken Kiev, of course. Eventually we stumbled out the door to our waiting gas vapor van to take us to the hotel. We were told by the grumbling driver, by way of our KGB friends, that dinner would start in precisely three hours. And it would begin with vodka toasts from some local dignitaries who wanted to meet us. Good Lord! It seems that word had gotten out about the Americans' visit to the tavern and how we were talking to babushkas, drinking vodka, and generally bonding with the local community.

After this experience, Bob's boundaries *really* came down. He felt like part of the Burba family, especially notable since he hadn't yet been accepted by some of his own family. It struck him that his life with Jim really was good for him (although maybe not for his liver). The positive feelings went both ways.

On the way home, at London's Heathrow airport, Ed pulled Jim aside. "Bob's good for you," he said. "You better hang on to him." This was huge for Jim. He respected his father immensely, and it was the first time his dad had ever said anything that openly validated both Jim's sexual identity and our relationship. It got Jim thinking even more seriously about our relationship. Up until then, Jim had been ready to commit, but he hadn't given a great deal of thought as to why, nor had he really been thinking about what the next fifty years of his life would look like. With his Dad weighing in, he could now see all that he had with Bob, and all that he would have.

Separate closets were now a thing of the past (although Bob did still label his clothes). We were fully committed—and we knew it. We had taken our time, gotten to know one another better, built trust, and allowed our feelings for one another to grow and mature. Since that trip to Russia, we've had our ups and downs, yet we've always stuck together. And as we've said, it's been worth it. In business and in life, truly committing to someone makes for a special relationship, one that means something precisely because of the commitments made and the sacrifices rendered. "I had a great relationship with Hervey," Tom Corcoran had told us. "I miss having someone I can go to and be completely open and candid with. I haven't yet been able to fill the void left by his death." With partnerships, it's clear: The more you give, the more you get. So be prepared to give a lot, on the first day and every day. Go all in.

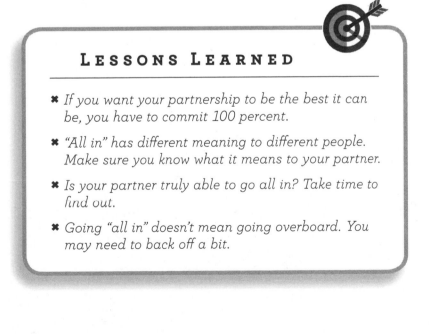

LESSONS LEARNED

* *If you want your partnership to be the best it can be, you have to commit 100 percent.*

* *"All in" has different meaning to different people. Make sure you know what it means to your partner.*

* *Is your partner truly able to go all in? Take time to find out.*

* *Going "all in" doesn't mean going overboard. You may need to back off a bit.*

CHAPTER SEVEN

Think Big, Start Small, and *Plan* for Success

Real estate investor and television personality, Donald Trump is nothing if not big. The man stands about 6´2˝ tall, is a billionaire many times over, and as of this writing an outspoken candidate in the 2016 presidential election. He is the owner or developer of soaring skyscrapers in a number of cities. "I like thinking big," he once said. "If you're going to be thinking anything, you might as well think big."

Many people don't think big when they enter into new partnerships. They might *dream* big, which is perhaps what Trump means. They imagine they will accomplish something important—building a successful business, creating an exciting new life for themselves, making a difference in the lives of others. But for all their ambition they often don't *think* big, in the sense of plotting strategically what might happen as their business develops. They're so jazzed about starting their venture that they don't plan for success or think rationally about their business' trajectory. As a result, a couple of bad things can happen. Sometimes they start out too big, embarking on an initial project that is overly complex, capital intensive, or risky. In short order, they flame out. Other times, they start modestly and find themselves struggling to adapt as their business gains momentum. In the best-case scenario, they experience a brush with death but manage to survive. In the worst-case scenario, well . . . let's not talk about that.

With our business, we fell into the second category—struggling to adapt. When we started Burba Hotel Network, we purposely started as small as possible by hiring ourselves out for a few small events that were fairly predictable and manageable. Not a lot of potential money, but a starting point. Resolved not to carry any debt, we managed our capital needs and lightened the logistical load by taking on a partner to launch our own event, which we thought could be big. We further mitigated our risks by having Jim keep a full time job outside our company. Because we did everything ourselves (e.g., bookkeeping, marketing, website design), and because Jim's employer gave us free office space, our overhead was extremely low, which helped keep our stress level down that first year and make our venture seem more practicable. We were paying our bills and even giving Bob a small salary so that he could make his car payment.

All this was smart partnering on our part. Unfortunately, we didn't extend that kind of careful thinking beyond the launch of our first owned event. Actually, that's a matter of some contention between the two of us. Jim contends that Bob did have a strategy in place—for *himself.* He had an escape clause that said that if he wanted to, he could bow out as a business partner after five years, no questions asked. Jim argues that while Bob had gone "all in" on their personal relationship after the babushka episode, it would take several years before he would go "all in" on their business partnership. This disparity actually caused Jim a good amount of stress, because as our business became established and growth opportunities arose, Jim wasn't sure whether we should accept them; he didn't know for certain if Bob would be around to help him run the business, and the company couldn't afford to bring someone in to replace him.

Bob contests Jim's version of the story. He thought that he was indeed "all in" on the business, even with the escape clause. We had worked out our agreement and playbook. That escape clause was there because of fear—Bob's fear of losing himself and his professional identity.

Jim's response to Bob: "So that means you weren't really all in!"

We can both agree that we didn't have any kind of business or financial plan in place specifying what we might do if our newest partnership and conference succeeded. Our approach was to "see how it goes"; we simply hoped we would make enough on that first new conference to pay the bills and fund subsequent conferences. We would judge ourselves successful if after the first year or so we had managed to stay solvent.

With the bar set so low, we wound up succeeding well beyond our expectations, walking away with enough money to cover our bills and also creating a bit of buzz in our industry. That was exciting, but we soon found our anxiety levels rising again. We hadn't appreciated a basic truth about our business: You're only as good as your last conference. As we now realized, our second conference had to be bigger and better than our first if we were to sustain our success. Meanwhile, people in our industry started coming to us with new opportunities. While this was immensely validating, we didn't have the capacity to execute more or bigger projects. We were still just the two of us and one employee. When we hired another employee to help us, the poor woman had to sit in a space the size of a closet because that was all Jim's employer had available.

Soon, we didn't even have that. About the time the big new event we launched was reaching its second year, we learned that Jim's employer would soon ask us to move our little company out of the office (big surprise there). They were growing and needed the space. We had very little notice and had to scramble to find new office space, right when we were franti-cally approaching the date of our event. We managed to find our first real office just in time, but then we realized that we had to acquire all the back-office infrastructure we had also been borrowing. What kind of computer system would we buy? Did we need a call answering system? Was it time to hire additional help? Could we afford it? What was the best way to finance all of this? We were playing catch-up with our busi-ness, all because we hadn't bothered to come up with some kind of strategy at the outset. We wound up improvising solutions as we went. It was unnecessarily stressful, and our solutions might not always have been the smartest and most economical. The lesson is this: Don't just wing it when embark-ing on a partnership, because you might not be as lucky as we were. Think big, start small, but *plan* for success.

FIND YOUR PLANNING SWEET-SPOT

We should have known better—or at least one of us should have. When Jim got his MBA, he learned all about the com-plex financial and business planning that legitimate companies do. Later, as a partner in his accounting firm, he saw the orga-nization do planning galore: Five year marketing plans, cap-ital plans, expenditure plans, growth plans, and so on. And yet, when it came to getting his own start-up off the ground, he failed to give the future much thought at all. Even today, we still don't do as much formal planning, budgeting, and so on as other companies our size. Our financial philosophy is "make the revenues grow over last year, and try to spend less."

Our lack of emphasis on planning is a mixed bag, and not necessarily something other partners should emulate. It often leaves us making decisions based on impulse, some of which don't work out. In chapter one, we recounted a global hotel magazine we helped start that didn't quite work out for us. We didn't join this venture because it fit neatly into a pre-existing strategic plan we'd crafted for our business. Rather, the business idea came our way, and it seemed like a good opportunity. Turned out it wasn't.

At around the same time, we wound up making an almost identical mistake with another venture. We formed a partnership with an old friend to provide organizations with strategic planning consulting and technology that allowed them to capture more meaningful information. Our thought was to sell this product to companies on our contact list. We didn't fully understand the market for this type of consulting, nor did we understand the product well enough to explain the virtues of digital meetings. We were in the business of marketing old-fashioned, face-to-face conferences. Not surprisingly, the venture didn't work out. We were dreaming big, but we weren't thinking it through and planning for success.

We don't want to be too hard on ourselves. Neither of these failures broke us, and we did come away with a greater sense of our own limitations. Other risks we've taken have panned out (read on for one of those). The way we see it, at least we're taking risks. We've moved our business forward and to date have avoided any major catastrophes.

A smaller company such as ours probably doesn't need, nor can it afford, the intricate planning processes that most large organization employ. Also, some partnerships may get along fairly well with less in the way of formal planning, simply because of the temperaments of the partners or the nature of their relationship. Because we're partners in our private life as well as business partners, we can be looser and more intuitive with budgeting and financial planning for our company. We do have to think about and plan for the future like anyone else, and our failures when we fail to strategize do sting. Yet we don't feel the same pressure that other partners might do to *report* our plans so that they are transparent to all the partners. We trust and respect one another, and in any given area of our business, each of us knows that the other is thinking in the same way.

When we partner with outside parties, or when we're operating in industries with which we're less familiar, we of course demand a much higher standard of rigor and scrutiny in our planning. We want to see budgets, and we want to understand in depth why they make sense. With our entertainment ventures, for instance, we ask a lot of questions. What are the project's capital needs now, and what will they be in six months or a year? What happens if a film project or a television show gets picked up by a major studio, and what happens if it doesn't? We trust our partners on these ventures, but we don't have the same history with them as the two of us, Bob and Jim, have with one another. We can't see inside our outside partners' brains. So we need to see the future of the business on paper, in black and white.

Our informal survey of other successful partnerships reveals some disparity when it comes to the extent and formality of planning. In 1987, at the age of 26, Chip Conley formed a new partnership that bought a motel in San Francisco's seedy tenderloin district and turned it into a cool boutique hotel. It would be the first successful acquisition among many for his well-known hotel company, Joie de Vivre Hospitality. As Chip told us, he did have a formal business plan, and it called for the company to own and run ten hotels within ten years (the company exceeded expectations, owning thirteen hotels by 1997). By contrast, fashion designer Trina Turk and her husband/partner Jonathan Skow were like us, more or less winging it at the outset. "I don't think I had a vision of what the company would be," Trina said. "I just wanted to do a nice little collection and do it myself, and not really have to answer to anybody. That was my main goal. I think it was really just about trying it, and you know, I talked about it for a long time before I actually quit my job and started. I never did any kind of business or financial plan, nor did we have any kind of clearly defined personal goals."

As these examples suggest, it's helpful to think about planning as a horizontal line, with no thought at all about the future at the far left, and detailed planning reports and endless planning meetings on the far right. We started much further to left than was healthy for our business. Today, having grown older and wiser, we're near the middle, although probably a little closer to the "less planning" side. Trina is probably in the middle as well, although closer to the "more planning" side. It's up to you to find your own sweet spot on the Planning Spectrum, a place that's comfortable and realistic for you, and not too close to either extreme.

Wherever your planning sweet spot is, it's important to have regular and ongoing discussions about the future of the partnership. Even if you've been good about framing strategies from the beginning, these discussions can confirm that you both still support the agreed upon strategies, and they can provide you an opportunity to revise your plans if market conditions have changed. Checking in can also help you uncover important disagreements about your vision for the company that may have gone unnoticed.

When Trina and Jonathan started their company, Trina was so busy that she had to bring in a colleague to help her with the production of her clothing line. In retrospect, Trina acknowledges that they should have hired this friend as an employee rather than making her a partner in the company, but "we were completely naïve at the beginning and didn't really know what we were doing." As the years ticked on, the new partner did a great job producing the clothing at the highest levels of quality. Yet it turned out that she had radically different ideas about what the company could become. Whereas Trina and Jonathan wanted to grow it, their partner wanted to keep it small, more "controllable."

"We had never really had a conversation with her about her goals," Trina relates, "so the differences between us kind of emerged over time." Trina eagerly took on responsibilities as the business grew, whereas their partner's responsibilities remained what they had initially been: making patterns for clothes and collaborating with the companies who manufactured their clothes. Disagreements arose over decisions large and small, and tension mounted. "She would literally say things like, "Well, I don't think we should hire any more people. Those are just more people who could sue us.'" Unfortunately, by this time, the company had grown so large that Trina and Jonathan couldn't afford to buy their partner out without taking on an uncomfortable amount of financial risk. They struggled on with their partner for years until a venture firm finally bought a 60 percent stake in the company, taking over their partner's share. Trina and Jonathan's conflict with their early partner ultimately didn't impede their company's growth, but if they could do it over, they would have had more thorough planning discussions up front.[15]

NOTCH EARLY WINS
TO BUILD CONFIDENCE

If you think big, start small, and plan for success, you put yourself in a position to gain momentum by notching early, manageable wins, which in turn can catapult you to ever-greater levels of success. In our case, our personal relationship was tried and tested by the time we started our business together, but we had no idea whether we'd be able to work well as business partners.

Would we bring our work home with us? Would we encroach on one another's responsibilities and authority? Would our skills and interests be as compatible with one another's as we had anticipated? What would it be like to see one another under stress in a professional environment? Would we have what it took to get the job done? The success of our first new conference taught us that we *could* win together, that we each had our role to play in the business, and that our partnership playbook worked well and didn't require significant revision.

More recently, we followed a similar approach when getting our entertainment business off the ground. Rather than betting everything on a big film project, we cast about for a relatively low-risk, slower way of getting into the business. Thinking strategically about the future, we decided that we wouldn't try to start up a project of our own, but rather attach ourselves to an existing project. From there, we would branch out to take on different kinds of entertainment projects once we had a little experience under our belts. The first film we helped produce, *Space Station 76*, was a perfect opportunity. The project's capital requirements were not overwhelming; if we lost our investment, it wouldn't be a huge blow. Because the project was already partially set up and underway by the time we became involved, we didn't have to go through the long process of finding a story, developing a script, becoming the lead producers, arranging the financing, finding the talent, hiring the crews, and driving everything else about the project. We could keep our existing business running and yet still learn from the process and see what it felt like to produce a film.

We kept our goals for this initial project modest. We wanted to see if entertainment was a good match for us, perhaps something that could take us into a different business direction in the years ahead. Of course, we wanted to earn back our investment, and if we made money on the deal, even better. Finally, we were "trying out" our partners on this deal, hoping that we might like working with them enough to attempt even bigger, more intensive collaborations. We were thinking big, like Academy Award-winner big, but we were starting small with manageable involvement and minimal financial risk on our part.

Although we didn't fully appreciate it at the time, the vast majority of independent films—as many as 90 percent—are poor financial investments that return little if any of the original capital. Happily, our project defied these frightening odds. A major film studio, Sony International, bought and distributed *Space Station 76* and this allowed us to earn our investment back. Depending on how many people view the film, we even stand to make a nice profit. During our work on the film, we developed a great relationship with the director, Jack Plotnick, and discovered that his creative vision was very close to ours. We also hit it off with the film's very efficient and professional production team. We have since signed on to produce a new Broadway show that Plotnick is directing, and our success on the film has given us the confidence to take on other kinds of projects with the production team, including the television show mentioned in an earlier chapter. Our exciting second business is off and running, all because we positioned ourselves to notch relatively easy wins and gain momentum.

A PLANNING CHECK-IN

Where do you and your partners stand on the Planning Spectrum? Do you take a more minimalist approach, like we do, or do you naturally tend to deliberate, document, and plot out your every future move? How good is your communication around planning? If you're a small business, do you make time for regular planning sessions, or do those never seem to happen? Once you've decided where you and your partners fall on the Spectrum, think about where you'd *like* to be. Should you collectively aim for more rigor, or should you try loosening up a bit more and taking some risks? Be honest. If you've failed on previous ventures, what role did poor planning play, and where precisely did your planning process fall apart? What blind spots did you and your partners fail to consider? What lessons can you glean about your risk-taking style?

If you're just embarking on a partnership, are you really starting small enough, giving yourself plenty of runway to notch some energizing wins? Is a failure going to send you into bankruptcy or saddle you with some other unfortunate long-term consequence? Be sure to compare your own risk-taking tendencies with those of your partner. It's helpful in any partnership for at least one party to be more risk-averse, and one to be more risk-prone. It's certainly part of our own balancing act, and a reason we've always taken *manageable* risks. Jim tends to have the big (and sometimes crazy) ideas, whereas Bob feels more comfortable being the "voice of no." Jim's vision takes us into uncharted territory; Bob's inclines us to slow down and think about the possible consequences if things don't work out. Most of the time, we agree on a course of action that satisfies both of us. Our failures, while they happen occasionally, pale in comparison to our successes.

We also try to stay alert to warning signs that we're *not* taking a measured, balanced approach to the future. For example, if you find yourself lurching from crisis to crisis and reacting to events or jeopardizing your core business to rush into something new, you might not have spent enough time thinking strategically about your future. Even if it feels like you can't spare a minute, take a half-day off with your partner for a planning retreat. Likewise, if you find yourself overwhelmed and cutting corners on quality, missing deadlines, or stressing out about the risks to your business, you might very well have started out too big. You should be able to survive a total failure of your initial venture; if not, then you're probably aiming too big. Keep all your ambitious, exciting dreams, but see if you can find ways of easing in slowly and notching a quick, affirming win.

A final piece of advice: When you do get that win, be sure to celebrate. We do it often. There really is nothing like a well-shaken martini to cement a partnership while also marking a job well done. But before that second or third martini, think through all that the partners in your venture contributed with a clear head, and all the healthy ways you worked together to make the magic happen.

GETTING SMART ABOUT GROWTH

Most marriages and business partnerships do begin with big dreams. Yet we make a mistake if we conflate dreaming big with actually thinking big about the future. It's okay to ride the wave of emotion when starting a partnership, but we say think analytically and strategically about your future, and allow for a trajectory of slow, manageable growth. Take your partnership one step at a time. Stay focused on small things you can accomplish. Calibrate your risks to assume a reasonable chance of failure. After all, you *did* learn to walk before you learned to run.

We have always learned the most from pushing ourselves and even more when we fall on our face. We don't fear failure; we embrace it as a learning exercise. But we need to remember as well that we can't do everything. By starting small, we lower the risk of an early flameout. No big dream, whether it's a building rising to the sky or making a movie about a Space Station, is worth pursuing if a potential failure will prove cataclysmic. Ambition may drive innovation in a partnership, but in the end your partnership's long-term survival is what matters most.

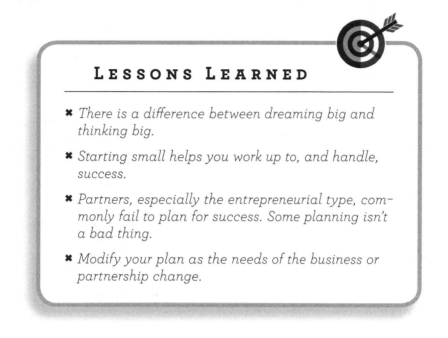

LESSONS LEARNED

* *There is a difference between dreaming big and thinking big.*

* *Starting small helps you work up to, and handle, success.*

* *Partners, especially the entrepreneurial type, commonly fail to plan for success. Some planning isn't a bad thing.*

* *Modify your plan as the needs of the business or partnership change.*

CHAPTER EIGHT

Play it Straight, Even When it's Tough

A few years ago, we were offered a chance to create an investment conference in a socially conservative Middle Eastern country. Our contact there was a businessman plugged in to the top levels of government. He was a good guy, honest, and well intentioned; he simply wanted to bring more tourism investment into his country. We were flattered and excited about what we saw as a lucrative business opportunity. We did wonder whether our sexual orientation would pose a problem in a society where women couldn't even show their faces, so we divulged our concerns to our contact. "That's okay," he said, "Just don't do anything that would embarrass us."

We took this to mean, "It's okay that you're gay—you just can't be open about it." We weren't offended by this stance; we understood it's important to respect cultural traditions. Yet the more we thought about it, the less comfortable we felt with the arrangement. Every time we traveled to the country, we'd have to go back into the closet, possibly bringing a "girlfriend" or "wife" along to social events for the sake of appearances. We normally keep a healthy boundary between our personal relationship and our professional engagements, but this kind of subterfuge seemed dishonest, to ourselves especially. Our lives were our lives. We live them openly. It didn't feel right to pretend to be something we were not, betraying principles we had worked hard to support and wholeheartedly believed in, such as respect, tolerance, openness, and equal rights. Although it was tough to turn down such an exciting opportunity and the money that would follow, we did precisely that. We stuck to our guns and played it straight—by refusing to play it straight.

A similar conundrum presented itself to us in 2014 when the Sultan of Brunei announced the harshest implementation of Sharia law in his country, including a provision that allowed for death by stoning of gay people. Boycotts erupted outside hotels the Sultan owned, including the Beverly Hills Hotel and the Dorchester London. We asked ourselves: What if the Dorchester brand wanted to sponsor our events as part of its growth strategy? Would it be the height of hypocrisy on our part to accept their money? We decided that we simply could not benefit financially from a company whose owner condemned our very existence. We had partnered for decades with a number of LGBT organizations to fight for equality, and we weren't going to nullify our work and that of so many others for the sake of profit. We removed Dorchester from our invitation lists and let our partners know about it.

In any partnership, situations will arise that challenge the partners' sense of right and wrong or threaten to compromise their integrity. We believe that in these situations, it is important to hew to the highest standards of ethical conduct, even if it means turning money away. In this era of entitlement, instant gratification, and naughty behavior, integrity sometimes seems hopelessly obsolete. Doing the wrong thing often seems to be doing the right thing. We don't buy this—at least, not when it comes to our business. Doing the right thing is the only way to operate, and for us at least, maintaining high levels of integrity has been crucial to the creation of enduring and successful partnerships.

In preaching integrity's merits, we realize that we run the risk of coming off as, well, preachy. Let's be clear: We're no choir boys (actually, Jim was one as a kid, but that's a different story). As gay men, we spent years of our lives in the closet, not disclosing important parts of ourselves to the world. We know what dishonesty feels like, and take it from us, it's not fun. That's precisely why we're so careful now to do the right thing in our business dealings. We don't want to go back to that bad old place, in any areas of our life. We sleep better playing by the rules, openly, and we also enjoy stronger commitments from the partners we do have.

We've seen firsthand what happens when we compromise integrity in our business dealings, even just a little bit. During our company's early days, we compromised on a special request from a sponsor who was also a key supporter and good business friend. Claiming to be in a tough spot financially, the sponsor begged us to lower what we charged for his company's participation in one of our conferences. If we cut the company some slack "just this once," our friend promised to come back the following year and pay the usual price. We were newbies at the time, hungry for revenues, so we agreed. We knew in our hearts that it wasn't fair to give this sponsor special treatment; all of this company's competitors were paying full price, and we had told all of our sponsors that everyone was getting the same deal.

The sponsor signed up and everything seemed great. However, the next year, the company conveniently forgot about the "we'll pay full price" commitment it had made. Pleading poverty again, it asked for the same special deal. We agonized over it but eventually turned the sponsor away. The sponsor got ticked off and dropped its sponsorship. Several years passed before they would even talk to us again about sponsoring. This was tough on us, as the sponsor was a big brand name in our industry. Lesson learned: If you bend the rules even once, it's hard to bend them back.

When your goal is to build strong, enduring partnerships based on trust, it's *always* better to be upfront, honest, and true to your beliefs. And it's best to do it out of a deeply felt concern for your partner's welfare. How will your partner fare if you're less than 100 percent honest, if you renege on your promises, or if you shirk your responsibilities hoping nobody will notice? Every day, we look at our actions both professionally and in our personal lives from that perspective. We care about our partners, and we care about the relationships we're building. The whole point of a partnership, we think, is to create an arrangement that allows *all* parties to reach desired and agreed-upon goals. It's a shared project, a joining together of individual interests to form a new, collective interest. If we're going to engage in deception—if we're willing to shortchange a partner and truly don't care about his or her or its wellbeing— why bother entering into the partnership in the first place?

THE VARIETIES OF "STRAIGHT" CONDUCT

We're not saying that all business partnerships should follow the same rules—in fact, they probably shouldn't. Industries, cultures, and individuals all differ, and what some might regard as an important matter of integrity, others might not. Some people might wish to run their businesses according to religious principles, for instance, while others might embrace more secular norms. Further, the religious-minded might wish to draw on any number of different religious traditions for guidance, leading them to adhere to very different ethical rules. What's important in all this is that partners agree on their own, joint codes of conduct, whatever those happen to be. Partners should have *something* clear and abiding to stick to. If they can't agree, that's a sign that entering into a partnership might not have been such a great idea.

Despite our largely relativist stance on ethical standards and rules, we would observe that some business precepts are so widespread as to be practically universal. For example, most people would equate "playing it straight" with a refusal to compromise on the quality of products or services, even when times get tough. Indeed, our research with other successful partners turned up many who regarded quality as inviolate. As furniture designer Mitchell Gold recounted, his rapidly growing company Mitchell Gold + Bob Williams was coping with the economic downturn in 2008.

At one point, a recently hired engineer, eager to help save the company money, announced that he had found a way to cut costs on packaging. Mitchell was pleased to hear this until he discovered, after the fact, that "cutting costs" meant significantly lowering the quality of the packaging. The company had heard from a few retailers and consumers about pieces that had arrived damaged because they hadn't been adequately protected. The company quickly put an end to this, reverting back to its previous packaging. "It reinforced to us what we already knew—that quality was critical to the brand, and we couldn't compromise it no matter what."[16]

We hold quality every bit as sacred as Mitchell and Bob do; the events we produce need to be up to standard, even when our own costs increase. But given the nature of our business, integrity for us has another focus that is even more important: Making sure we never, ever play favorites. It isn't just about charging sponsors or delegates the same rates; it's about making sure *every* decision we make about our events is equitable and transparent to vendors, customers, and everyone else we touch. If we give a speaker from one company a more attractive time slot at an event, we balance it by doing the same thing for their competitor the following year. If we feature one company's CEO as a speaker one year, we feature a competitor's the following year. We actually keep track of these details to ensure fairness. We like to say that, "We aim to be Switzerland. We're neutral." We don't take sides, nor do we play competitors off one another. We make our neutrality known as a key feature of doing business with us, and we make sure our partners, present and future, are all on the same page with this way of working.

Other industries function very differently. In the media world, a lot of wheeling and dealing goes on around the sale of advertising. A publication might tell a customer that the cost of an ad is, say, $10,000, but if the customer buys two other kinds of ads, that price goes down to $7,000 or less, depending on how well the customer negotiates or how badly the publication wants to make a sale. At car dealerships, sales people feel pressure to meet their goals, routinely cutting customers special deals because they happen to come in at a time of the month when they're desperate to do deals.

We're not dismissing the business practice of negotiating on price. It's expected and considered "normal" in these cases, and that's fine. It just doesn't feel like the best way to run *our* business. We care about everyone with whom we work; we aim to treat customers like partners and we don't think one is better than another. We want them *all* to have a fair shake. We also recognize that neutrality is in our interest. The global hotel business is a lot smaller than it sounds. Only a handful of global players truly dominate—Hilton, Hyatt, Marriott, Wyndham, Best Western, Choice, Accor, and a few others. If we were to play favorites, word would spread, and we would alienate some of these major players. Since we don't play favorites, we've developed a reputation over time as straight shooters who keep the industry's best interests at heart. People who do business with us know that they're getting the same deal as everyone else. They might not like it all the time, but they know that they can trust us. Their loyalty follows in due course.

Treating everyone equally according to the same transparent rules has other benefits. We can create standard "playbooks" for each event we produce that lays out what participants receive, what they pay for it, and how various processes and procedures will work. The events work much more smoothly and with less drama because everyone is clear about the rules, and nothing needs to be negotiated last-minute. And because there's less drama, people are happier being involved with our events. They don't have to spend as much of their own time monitoring the treatment their competitor is getting so as to jockey for position. They can sleep well at night knowing that they got a fair deal.

"TOUGHIES" RULE!

"Playing it straight" is a kind of discipline—the discipline of saying *no*. As we've seen, "No!" isn't a bad word when negotiating with prospective partners, and it's not a bad word to use with customers, vendors, or anyone else with whom you might be doing business and whom you might consider as informal "partners." Contrary to conventional wisdom, the customer *isn't* always right—in fact, nobody is. Whenever anyone asks you to take actions that conflict with your beliefs and principles, they're wrong, and you owe it to yourself and to them to stay strong. Otherwise, you'll keep bending the rules and over time there won't be *any* rules.

In our industry, some people call us the "toughies." In fact, our Asia event partners first gave us that label. They know we're ready and able to say no—they expect it. When we decline customer or partner requests to bend the rules, they'll say, "I knew that's what you'd say, but I at least had to ask."

Whether it has to do with ethics or any other kind of negotiation, saying "no" can be excruciating. When we first became
involved with one of our overseas events, we set about trying to find a new, big-league sponsor. A large global financial services firm expressed interest. Awesome! It seemed like
this was the breakthrough we needed to make our event more
upscale. It took forever for us to get the paperwork processed,
but finally the clock had run out and the contract was ready for
the sponsor to sign. At five in the afternoon West Coast time,
our fax machine started to ring—the contract was finally here!
Just as we were ready to pop the champagne, we took a closer
look at the document that had come through. Incredibly, the
sponsor had taken the contract we'd sent, made a number of
significant changes that benefitted them at our expense, and
typed it up to look as if it was the exact same document we had
sent. They had signed this document, not the one we'd agreed
on. At first glance, we didn't notice it was totally re-typed.

OMG! We picked up the phone and called Asia. We were
trembling with anxiety. We couldn't accept the contract they
wanted. We had to risk losing them as sponsors. We would
have to say no. And that's exactly what we did. "Excuse me," we
said to the woman on the sponsor's side, "you can't just go mod-
ifying terms that we've already agreed on and pass it off as the
document we sent to you. If you want to do business with us,
you'll have to sign and send us the original contract that we had
both accepted." We couldn't believe we were saying this to the
sponsor of our dreams.

There was a pause. "Well," said the woman, "we figured as
much, but we thought we'd try to negotiate a little more anyway. Give me two minutes. I'll get you the original document."

We looked at one another in amazement. We had said
no, and had been prepared to suffer the consequences. Happily, there wouldn't be any consequences with this sponsor/

partner—the deal went through. But the episode affirmed for us what we were capable of doing, and how willing we were to walk away when an occasion demanded it. We felt more confident knowing that in the heat of the moment, we had stuck by our guns. This episode has affected how we do deal with any dilemma we face. It's made us stronger, so that today we hesitate even less before doing the right thing. We've made the hard decisions in the past—we know what that feels like. We're willing to do it again.

In his book *You Can't Lead with Your Feet on the Desk*, longtime Marriott executive Ed Fuller describes a time when a partner in China wanted to cut corners when building a Marriott-branded hotel. The building had been built, and during the construction process the local Chinese partner had lost control over his own vendors, resulting in a shoddy final product. Marriott had to decide whether or not to accept the building. It wasn't easy entering new global markets; it required a lot of time and energy cultivating relationships with local business partners. Rejecting the building would jeopardize the relationship with this Chinese partner and perhaps make future deals unlikely. On the other hand, Marriott had its global brand name to consider. If guests experienced any mishaps or safety issues, Marriott would ultimately bear responsibility. The company did the right thing and rejected the building, refusing to open it until it was constructed up to its standards. "We did this in many, many cases," Fuller told us in an interview. "Construction outside the United States wasn't well regulated, and we really had to hold the line on the quality of our products. We had to insist on our standards and convince our partners that there was a line in the sand beyond which we would not go."

In this instance, some tough conversations followed. Marriott battled the Chinese partner for some time, knowing that it could lose part or all of its investment, since legal contracts were not as enforceable in China as they were in the United States. Eventually the construction problems were fixed, with Marriott giving in on a few minor, cosmetic issues. The partner came to appreciate that Marriott was doing the right thing by maintaining the integrity of its construction standards, even if he had to pay a bit more in construction costs.

Most everyone who has accomplished anything over time has had to be a "toughie" at times. Yet there are limits to this. Although in many situations the rule is often the rule, in others there is more of a grey area, and partners might not need to take such a hard line. Also, you and your partner(s) don't all have to be "toughies" when dealing with outside parties. In our case, one of us is temperamentally "tougher" than the other (we'll let you guess who that is). The "good cop" among us can emphasize to an outsider how much he wishes we could accede to that special request, softening the blow when the "bad cop" among us (okay, it's Bob) says no. Outsiders might see us as tough overall, but they know that we're not entirely inflexible or unfeeling. Finding partners that complement your toughness or softness and that share your commitment to specific ethical principles can help you achieve a nice balance.

OUR TOP FIVE WAYS
WE PLAY IT STRAIGHT

Playing it straight is simple in theory, but it can be tricky in its execution. During hard economic times, it's tempting to succumb to pressure and compromise your principles. There's no way around the discipline that a commitment to ethics requires, but over the years we've taken some actions that have helped make sticking to principles easier and less messy.

+1+

Have a "values" conversation early on with your partner, preferably before you lock in the partnership. Make values part of the courtship process. Most of the time you can get a feel for how a prospective partner might do business, but you ideally will enter a partnership explicitly agreeing on your joint principles. If you talk values and beliefs early on, you'll be able to refer back to that initial conversation when challenging situations arise. You'll make better, more thoughtful decisions because you won't be having that initial conversation under pressure. Also, you will have established values as an important part of the culture of your partnership.

If you and your partner are clearly aligned around values from the outset, you can also count on your partner to hold you accountable (and vice versa). As Mitchell Gold told us, his partner Bob does that for him, and he greatly admires him for it. Once in the early days of their business, Mitchell was in their showroom selling furniture to a customer when Bob pulled him aside. "Why did you just do that?"

"Do what?" Mitchell asked.

"When you were explaining the benefits of the furniture, you exaggerated it."

Mitchell shrugged. "I don't know. I didn't mean to. It just sounded better."

"But you didn't need to exaggerate. So why did you do it?"

Bob was right; Mitchell had unnecessarily exaggerated in his sales pitch ever so slightly. "It was such a minor transgression," Mitchell told us, "in fact, arguably not even a transgression. It was silly. Yet the fact that Bob pointed that out to me, well, that just showed me once again his level of integrity. I was grateful for the reminder, and grateful all over again to have him as my partner."

+2+

Make your partnership's ethical principles and practices clear to the outside world at all times. If people in your world know your policies, they'll have proper expectations. Many will be inclined not to challenge them, but when some people do, you'll be in a better position to say "no." Think of all those signs at public swimming pools that list the twenty-five things you're *not* allowed to do. Sure, when you were a kid all those rules equaled one thing: No fun. But because you knew them, the lifeguard could say "no running!" and it didn't come as a big surprise. You didn't argue about the rule. You just did what the lifeguard said.

+3+

Have an answer ready if people ask you to compromise your values. When people request inappropriate favors from us, we take the direct approach in brushing them off. A simple "we're sorry, but we can't do that" is most likely the answer. If the pressure is on or we get significant push back, Jim will respond, "Are you asking me to compromise our integrity?" He makes apparent the true stakes of the seemingly trivial request, changing the whole tenor of the conversation. Typically, the people making these requests won't push for them any further. Nobody wants to ask someone else to compromise his or her integrity, because that implicitly suggests that they themselves don't have any.

We know that we'll likely be asked for special favors in the weeks immediately preceding one of our big events. People whom we haven't spoken with in months or years will call, ostensibly to "check in" and ask if there's anything they can do to "help" us. What follows is a request for freebies, a last-minute break in price, an extra admission pass, or a room at a sold-out hotel. So here's what we do. Right before an event, whenever we field a call from someone we haven't talked to in a while, before he even gets a chance to tell us why he is calling, we'll take the initiative and say, "Hey, good to hear from you, and yeah, it's crazy around here. We're really busy with the event coming up. And we're getting all these weird phone calls now where people are asking us for special favors. That's the biggest thing we deal with now, all these strange last minute requests. So, what's up?" An awkward silence ensues, and then the caller will say something like, "it was good talking with you, I just wanted to check-in and see how you were doing." This works great for us.

✦4✦

Go back and read chapter five. Why? Because that's where we talked about the partnership playbook. The more you concretize your principles into specific rules for each formal or informal partner, the less room you're leaving for uncertainty about what your principles mean and how they might be applied. You and the partners and your outside collaborators will be more aligned, and disagreements will be minimized.

✦5✦

Listen to that part of you located at belt-level. We're talking about your gut. We all intuitively know the difference between good and bad, right and wrong. We might not always *want* to know, but we do. Perform a gut check for your more challenging ethical quandaries. If you think something doesn't sound quite right, it probably isn't. Pay attention if you don't have a quick, easy answer to a request or proposal someone makes. If you have to think hard about what to do, chances are you're being asked to compromise a belief or principle. Rather than offering an answer on the spot, make a practice of telling people, "I'll get back to you." Give yourself the time you need to think the situation through and perform a thorough gut-check.

HOLDING THE LINE AND BUILDING TRUST

Making an effort to play it straight really does pay off. One of the best illustrations of this that we've encountered comes from Marriott's Ed Fuller. He told us of the time when Marriott entered into a joint venture to build a hotel in Shanghai. A local developer owned the hotel, and Marriott received a licensing fee as well as a fee to oversee the property's operations. At one point several years after the hotel had opened, the hotel's general manager was caught committing a small indiscretion; he had inappropriately expensed $300 in personal costs. It wasn't a big deal—most companies probably would have shrugged it off, especially since the general manager was a high performer and on track for a promotion. Yet Fuller had him terminated "on the premise that there are no secrets in a hotel and that we had to take steps to ensure transparency and the quality of Marriott's management."

The story seemed to have ended there, but there was a surprise coda. About six months later, Marriott's legal team spotted an error in the Chinese version of its management contract for the hotel. It said that the contract would stay in force for only ten years, not the twenty years that the parties had agreed to. That ten-year period was almost up. Marriott went back to the local owner with its hat in its hand, ready for arduous negotiations over its management fees. If the owner had wanted to, he could have demanded that he pay much lower fees to Marriott for the final ten years, among other concessions. Marriott would have had to comply or risk losing the management contract. Yet those negotiations never happened. "The owner looked at us and said, 'Look, it is hard to find people in this industry, in this world, that you can trust. I never thought you'd fire the GM for that $300 infraction, but since you did, it helped me begin to trust you more.'" The owner scratched out the error on the Chinese contract and wrote in ten more years.

Legal contracts people sign often don't mean very much. What does mean something is your word, and your word takes on even more weight if it is consistently reinforced by *actions*. Play it straight, and your partners will do the same. Deviate from your principles, and your partners—the best of them, anyway—will flee. Integrity isn't obsolete, even in our crazy day and age. Trust still undergirds relationships of any kind, and nothing builds trust more than a consistent record of adhering to one's deeply felt ethical principles. As preachy as it sounds, when you stick to what's right, others will notice and respect you for it. Integrity is the basis for our strong partnerships and always will be.

LESSONS LEARNED

* *Integrity may be the most important asset a business or partnership possesses.*

* *Being "Switzerland" is the right thing to do, and it actually makes your life easier.*

* *Partners need to agree on and follow a common code of conduct.*

* *Customers may not always like it, but ultimately they respect you for playing consistently by the rules.*

CHAPTER NINE

A Little More Facetime, a Little Less Facebook

Do you meet regularly with your partners? What about with your less formal, partner-style relationships? When problems or challenges arise, is your first inclination to get together in person to talk it through?

If you answered "no," or even a hesitant "yeah, sort of," then this chapter is for you. Good, old-fashioned face-to-face time is becoming increasingly rare in our globalized, Facebook-friendly world. People love their devices, and they seem to think that smartphones, tablets, smart watches, and the like give them everything they need to stay in touch and connected. But they *don't*. Not even close. As wonderful as technology is, email, social media, and texting are impersonal. Users of these technologies miss important factors like the look on a person's face, her body language, and subtle inflections in her voice. Technology also promotes sound bites of communication rather than deeper connections and exchanges of nuanced ideas. It prevents us from truly concentrating on what others are saying, and from creating safe spaces for others to express themselves and bring out their best thinking. Studies have shown that even the mere presence of a smartphone in the room inhibits the formation of relationships.[17]

In our business, we prioritize regular, in person contact—
it's one of our fundamental partnership principles. Bringing
together thousands of travel professionals each year in our
conferences, we've seen first-hand just how powerfully personal contact builds trust. We've also discovered that people
require *more* regular, face-to-face contact as information technology advances, not less. Although millennials are commonly
thought of as obsessed with their gadgets, that doesn't necessarily hold true at work; studies have found that majorities
of millennials surveyed preferred in-person conversations in
their workplaces.[18] As *Joie de Vivre* founder and Airbnb executive Chip Conley observes, "The more digital we get as a society, the more we need the ritual of putting our gadgets down
and having that facetime directly. It's the difference between
'URL' and 'IRL.' A URL, of course, is a website. IRL is *in real
life*. And In Real Life matters."

You can make the most of your partnerships by balancing
out the URL and the IRL. Check in regularly with partners. Ask
real questions and listen carefully to what your partners are saying. Relish the opportunity to get to know your partners better,
live and in the flesh. That's what we've done (with a few martinis
added in for good measure), and it has helped. We're not talking
about a monumental shift here, just a slight change in emphasis.
When it comes to building trust in any relationship, a little more
facetime, a little less Facebook can make all the difference.

MEETINGS BEHIND THE MEETINGS

We first became attuned to the importance of facetime when
creating our early events. We wanted to plan conferences so
that the content was as fresh and relevant to our industry as
possible, yet we weren't sure how to mobilize the best thinking. Jim remembered how earlier in his career he had helped

bring together some of his accounting firm partners to brainstorm about certain topics. Since most of these partners had similar backgrounds and presented the same perspectives, the sessions tended to yield only boring, conventional ideas. His firm simply couldn't think beyond the walls of its office, and it showed. Drawing on that experience, we realized we needed to go outside our company and collaborate with others in the hospitality industry to plan our events. We would have to bring key players together face-to-face around a table so that they could help us create the events that *they* wanted.

We devised a new planning process. Nine months before our annual event, we gathered sponsors and key individuals with content expertise for a day or two to brainstorm about what the event might look like. The idea was to create a planning meeting where the "customer" (our informal partner) was given the ability to create the actual product. We had all angles of the industry covered: Lawyers, consultants, brokers, architects, finance people, developers, and hotel company executives. There was no pressure at this meeting, no sales pitch from us, and no lobbying by participants on behalf of their organizations for perks or visibility at our conference. Rather, we were all there for a free and fun exchange about industry trends and the content at our conferences that would best convey them.

The benefits of this process to our business were evident immediately and continue to this day. Because key industry players felt they had a voice, they become more engaged in our events, seeing themselves as partners, not merely sponsors. Their loyalty deepened, and they enthusiastically spread the word about our events to their networks of industry contacts. Meanwhile the ideas we came up with together were far better than anything the two of us could have developed working alone. We came away with a whole new vantage point on our industry. For anyone who wanted to learn about where the hospitality industry is headed, our events were the place to be. And that was precisely because of the facetime we put in at our planning meetings.

It gets better. Much to our delight, executives at our sponsoring companies have come to see one another as partners. These executives are in many cases direct competitors. They might encounter one another at industry events, including ours, but on those occasions they aren't able to build personal connections because they are rivals, always chasing the same deals. Our planning meetings are often the first chance they have to come together and develop friendships. Participants compare notes and commiserate on shared challenges. They get to know their competitors as *people*. They discover that their competitors face the same issues they do in growing their businesses, and that there are things they can all do together to help one another and the entire industry grow and develop.

We should emphasize that these meetings are also fun. At a recent planning session in Dallas, Texas, we took planning participants on VIP tours of the Dallas Cowboys football stadium and then treated them to a traditional Texas barbecue dinner. At one planning session in Los Angeles some time ago, our group all went bowling at Lucky Strike lanes in Hollywood. Who showed up for people watching was none other than Teri Hatcher, one of the stars of the then hit TV show *Desperate Housewives*. On still another occasion, we arranged for a sunset volleyball game at beautiful Malibu beach, with cocktails of course.

Bringing customers together to help plan your product is hardly an innovative business technique. Yet when we first began these meetings, none of our competitors were doing it. Even today, some don't, and those that do haven't made their planning meetings as collaborative as ours are. As a result, those meetings don't produce the same exchange of ideas that ours do, nor do they build relationships as strongly. Our planning meetings remain unique, and we think they're one the biggest reasons our events have been so successful and long-lived.

TECHNOLOGY ALONE CAN'T HACK IT

"C'mon," you're saying, "interacting in person is great, but time and money are short. Can't we email or videochat and get basically the same results?" Usually the answer is no. On a couple of occasions, we sought to cut costs by holding planning meetings online (actually, it was Bob, the most cost-conscious of the two of us, who proposed this). The result? Our virtual planning meetings weren't nearly as successful. Participants were distracted in their offices, handling emails, reading documents, and talking with their staff at the same time as they were supposed to be interacting with us. The flow of the conversation became stunted because of how difficult it usually is to hear when multiple people speak at the same time over an Internet platform. Because participants couldn't see one another's emotional reactions as well as in person, they couldn't connect as well and relax enough to share their ideas as openly.

We've experimented with offering some of our conference content as online webinars. The technology allows us to know when participants are touching their keyboards and when they're active on their screens. We found that as many as 75 percent of participants weren't actively engaged by the end of the session. They weren't adding input on their keyboard. They weren't toggling. They weren't asking questions. They weren't doing much of anything. Was our content the culprit? We would have thought so—except participants had found this same content deeply engaging during our in-person sessions. It was the technology. Facetime allows people to engage, whereas technology makes it much easier to remain a passive observer, or even to tune out entirely.

Technological interactions are so common and seemingly efficient that many don't even realize how relatively impoverished they can be. If you want to get something done, or if you want to get the best, most creative thinking out of someone, you can't do it remotely. You have to *be there*.

You'll remember that our company got started because Tony Marshall, a former professor and the head of a hospitality education association, advised Jim that he should start a business of his own. There's an important backstory there. Jim had known Tony for years as a business acquaintance, having talked with him on the phone many times and even interacting briefly with him at conferences. Jim realized that he was going to be in Orlando, where Tony was based, so he took the opportunity to meet with Tony for a relaxed lunch, simply for the purpose of getting to know him better. It was during that lunch that Tony casually communicated his advice to Jim and even suggested a future collaboration between his organization and Jim's then-hypothetical company. It's stunning to us to think how this one, in-person encounter gave rise not merely to our business, but to our most successful conference event. What if Jim hadn't taken the extra time to build this relationship?

Despite the great promise of social media, it's also harder with technology alone to forge connections with *friends* of your friends. Bob has a habit of looking to meet people so that he can meet the people they know—as he terms it, the "people behind the people." He likes to say, "everyone you know knows someone you should know." It's a classic cocktail party strategy, and because he applies it consistently in person, he has truly gotten to know and partner with some wonderful people.

One of our best examples involves Lorna Luft, Judy Garland's daughter and Liza Minelli's sister. She lives in Palm Springs and is a good friend of Kevin Bass, one of our good friends. Kevin had been trying to connect us; Judy Garland had been a lifelong friend of Johnny Mercer, and we own his former house in Palm Springs, so Kevin thought we'd have some fun talking. We became Facebook friends with Lorna, but a meeting never materialized. Finally, we attended a charity benefit where they were raffling off prizes, including a "lunch with Lorna." Bob bought a ticket and won lunch with Lorna, and from there we developed a friendship with her.

This is where the story gets good. A year or so later, Lorna was receiving an award that we had been happy to sponsor. To help make sure she enjoyed some facetime with her friends and admirers before the award dinner, we hosted a cocktail party for her at our house. We invited some of our friends, and she invited some of hers. One of her friends was the Broadway writer and actor Seth Rudetsky. One of *his* good friends, whom he brought along, was an actor named Jack Plotnick, whom Bob vaguely recognized. It turned out he had been on the original *Ellen Show, Buffy the Vampire Slayer*, the film *Gods and Monsters*, and other shows Bob had seen. Because Bob asks a lot of questions, he discovered that Plotnick was working on a new movie called *Space Station 76*.

And that's how we came to become involved in our first movie venture. Our commitment to facetime allowed us to make connections that turned into an important business partnership for us, thanks of course to subsequent facetime experiences. We might have become the most casual "friends" with Plotnick had we sifted through Lorna Luft's friends on Facebook and "friended" him. But we never would have gotten to know him and laid the foundation for a meaningful and lasting partnership.

SPEED IT UP!

The benefits of in-person contact seem so obvious, so why don't people do it more? Clearly facetime isn't as efficient; it takes more time and money. But there's another reason. For many people, in person interactions are just *harder*. It's scarier to sit across from a person and actually talk than it is to type into a keyboard and perhaps see them on a screen. What questions do you ask? How do you respond to the other person's questions? What's "safe" to say and what isn't? What if you say something "stupid"? These questions seem even more vexing as people become habituated to technology. They lose touch with the basic social skills they learned in kindergarten, forgetting how to forge real relationships. They become afraid to even try. As a result, they miss out on chances to forge relationships that could one day become enriching partnerships.

Sometimes the only thing people need in order to overcome their fears and engage with one another human being is a little push. This brings us to something fun we do called "speed meet." One night Jim couldn't sleep, so he turned on the TV to find that an old comedy show rerun was playing. One of the characters was recently single, so she went to a speed dating event to meet people. She sat across from the table, meeting a series of men and exchanging phone numbers along the way. It was a safe, fun, relaxed way to meet a date. A light bulb lit up in Jim's head: Our customers, the people who attend our conferences, need something just like this. Not that they come to our conferences looking for dates. But in a way, they do. They're looking to form possible relationships with people, relationships that could turn into long-lasting, profitable business partnerships. Some of our customers are stymied because they have trouble starting up meaningful conversations.

In 2006 we introduced "speed meet." Participants get three minutes to talk to another person about anything. Boom—on to the next person for another three minutes. In the space of an hour, each participant has now officially made friends with twenty fellow industry professionals they otherwise might never have gotten to know. If you find yourself stuck having a challenging or awkward conversation, no worries—you only have to suffer for 180 seconds. If you do hit it off, great: You can exchange business cards and continue the conversation later. We do speed meetings at the beginning of conferences, *before* the usual meet-and-greet cocktail party. Guess what? That cocktail party is much more vibrant and fun. The conference as a whole gets off to great start.

Hundreds of people show up for speed meet; they're among our most popular programs. Even some industry veterans attend—the people you'd least expect would lack confidence in social situations or who have a need to meet new people. It just goes to show: everybody can use a little more facetime.

INVEST IN YOUR PARTNERSHIPS

When it comes to in-person interactions, partnerships are kind of like those prized hydrangea you might have in your garden. Those fabulous flowers need lots of water and loving-kindness when you first drop them in the ground. But they need even more water and loving kindness throughout the season and then again every season. Otherwise, the poor hydrangeas will wilt and die. Likewise, in-person interaction can't just happen once or twice at the beginning of a partnership. You have to keep doing it to ensure that the partnership stays strong and is forever deepening.

Bruce Chemel knows a thing or two about consistent, long-term "facetiming." For a decade starting in 1991, the former

President of the American Airlines AAdvantage rewards program oversaw important partnerships the program maintained with participating vendors. These vendors—credit card companies, rental car companies, hotel brands—bought large numbers of miles each year to award their own customers for their loyalty. Chemel needed to keep them excited about the program so that they showed it loyalty and didn't defect to a competing airlines rewards program. As Chemel recalls, he and his team relied on a regular regime of facetime to maintain their partnerships. They held large partner meetings every year for the purpose of showing their appreciation and filling partners in on the latest news relating to the AAdvantage program.

For the program's most important partners, Chemel went even further. He dedicated an entire team to his largest partner, Citibank, making his colleagues available to meet with Citibank executives as often as they liked. "You have to be in constant communication," Chemel told us. "You have to understand their needs, be accommodating, and be very responsive. As our program grew, the most senior executives at American Airlines took greater interest and met personally with Citibank's chief officers. That's how important the business was."

With smaller but still significant partners, Chemel's group couldn't devote an entire team to manage the relationships, but he still made significant accommodations. AAdvantage would give car and hotel companies marketing information about its passengers, allowing them to maximize the value they got out of the AAdvantage program. The program also generated special promotional ideas for them to help them with their marketing efforts. "The facetime was very, very important," Chemel remembered. "Our partners loved meeting with me, and they liked the ideas I would bring them. We had fun. I would take our partners often to sporting events—the socializing built bridges. We would also visit some of our partners every year, meeting privately with them. These partner conferences were also very important, an opportunity to develop good personal relationships with some of the smaller partners that I personally didn't have time to meet with during the year, even if my staff did."

Chemel's reliance on in-person interaction required a significant outlay of time and money. But American Airlines looked at it as an investment, one that was well worth making. How else would AAdvantage understand the changing businesses of its partners and keep its own goals aligned with theirs?

So many companies large and small understand their partners in dated or overly superficial ways, simply because they don't bother to check in regularly and listen. You need the time to ask open-ended questions and let conversations meander, or to probe more deeply into a part of their experience or their business that you hadn't considered. Over time, that's what our own planning sessions have allowed us to do. Year after year, we check in with our event sponsors to get an updated sense of their objectives. This gives us a chance to come up with solutions for their problems before our competition does, and sometimes before our sponsors even know they need a solution.

You might object that your business is global and you really can't afford to spend all your time meeting with customers, suppliers, and so on. We totally get that. Our business is global, too. We're not able to meet with all of our sponsors and business partners as often as we'd like. Still, we do our best to meet face-to-face as often as we can—*before* a problem arises that requires personal interaction to fix. Sometimes we'll tag on an extra day or two to a trip just to meet with sponsors in a given city in order to build the relationships. We'll make a point of asking questions and listening, not talking. We'll ask all kinds of questions, including personal ones, the kinds of things you might not feel comfortable asking in an email. We'll pay attention to cultural sensitivities and seek to learn about their cultures. We'll take note of the nuances—an inflection in a person's voice, their facial expressions. The important thing is to make the effort, to show that you care, to pay attention. This chapter advocates a little more facetime, a little less Facebook. Not a lot. Just a little.

BE THERE WHEN IT COUNTS

In January 2011, Ed Fuller was sitting in a corporate staff meeting at Marriott's offices in Washington, DC when an urgent message came through. Violent unrest had broken out across Egypt, events that would come to be known as part of the "Arab Spring." Marriott had seven hotels in the country and two more under construction, along with some 4,000 employees. There was no telling what might happen in the days to come, and whether any of those employees might be at risk.

Executives at other companies might have hunkered down in their offices and watched events unfold at a safe distance. Not Marriott's executives. Fuller jumped into action, flying to Cairo via Dubai. His mission on behalf of Marriott's most senior executives was to visit each of the hotels, listen to the stories of local staff members, and offer reassurance that Marriott's corporate leadership was 100 percent behind them. He would also spend time in the hospitals visiting wounded employees if necessary and meeting with authorities to help secure Marriott properties and the interests of Marriott's partners and employees.

Fuller had taken trips like this before under crisis conditions—many times, all over the world. Typically, he met with the hotel's security team and walked around the hotel, assessing the situation. Then he met with local owners of the hotel (Marriott was licensing its brand and managing the hotel in exchange for a fee from the local businessmen who actually owned the hotel property), reassuring them that Marriott would stand by them. He went around the hotel and shook hands with as many associates as possible. Finally, he met with the hotel's executive team and department heads to talk about the issues they faced—did they have enough food on hand? What were their families going through? Was there any way Marriott could help?

When he got to the company's large Cairo property, it seemed secure enough; Fuller found it surrounded by tanks and armored personnel carriers. Before spending a lot of time talking to staff, he decided to fly to another part of the country to visit the Marriott properties there. When he returned to the Cairo property the next day, he was surprised to find the hotel's executive team, all Egyptians, standing outside the property waiting for him. They had quite a story to tell. While Fuller had been gone, the Minister of the Interior had ordered all police removed from the hotel and its vicinity. A competing hotel chain's local leadership had abandoned its properties out of fear that crowds of rioters would break in and loot the hotel. The Marriott property was housing 600 guests at the time, including Western journalists, so the leadership team had been especially afraid of being targeted. Rather than flee, they and hotel employees stood strong and provided for their own security. The executive chef came up with the solution: He and his team grabbed their cleavers and stood behind the security officers at the three gates. The housekeeping staff joined in, equipped with brooms, axes, anything else they could wield as improvised weapons, while the engineers lent a hand, armed with shovels. Together, they stood guard and held the crowds at bay for four hours until the military arrived to secure the area. The hotel had tried to call Fuller to let him know about the situation, but his cell phone hadn't been working.

When Fuller told us this story, we didn't understand at first what his function was on the ground. Why had he bothered to fly into a city convulsed by unrest? Was it really necessary to brave the danger? As he told us, it was necessary. "The principle we lived by was that if there was any kind of serious incident, whether unrest or a bombing, anything at all anywhere in the world, we needed to be there in person to shore up morale. A key executive from corporate needed to be there, and quite often, that was me." It was all about taking care of the people on the ground, showing them that they weren't just numbers to the team back in corporate. "We were asking these associates on the ground to staff our hotels in these tough environments. As leaders, we needed to step up, too. It's part of the Marriott culture—take care of your associates, and they'll take care of the customer. And the customer will keep coming back."

As Fuller attested, showing up in the toughest of times invariably made an impression, rebounding to the company's benefit. "Whenever we went into a crisis, whether it was Egypt, Pakistan, or Jakarta, everybody in the local community came away knowing we were there for them. They knew we weren't just looking after our American employees—we were looking after every one of our partners. That built in a level of trust that helped us in any number of subsequent dealings. People realized that we personally cared about them. You just can't communicate that using Facebook."

Social media may be here to stay, but frequent personal contact remains critical to a good partnership. At an extreme, the most heroic among us will show up in person to help during a crisis situation. Yet you don't need to risk your life trekking to the next global hot spot, like Fuller so admirably did. Try just stopping in on an ordinary day and saying hello. Try scheduling special meetings every quarter or every year, or sneaking in extra days on business trips for that casual beer, that round of golf, that relaxed lunch. If your partner lives on the other side of the world and you simply can't meet in person, try spending more quality time on the phone, talking about personal stuff as well as business. Make it clear to your partners that your relationship matters. As we've found, small gestures like these can make all the difference.

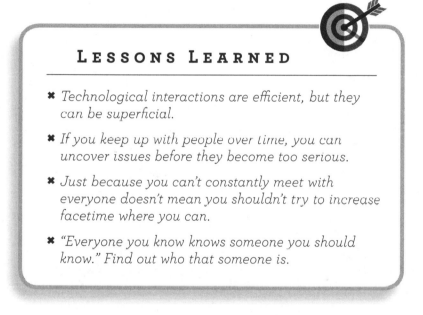

LESSONS LEARNED

* *Technological interactions are efficient, but they can be superficial.*

* *If you keep up with people over time, you can uncover issues before they become too serious.*

* *Just because you can't constantly meet with everyone doesn't mean you shouldn't try to increase facetime where you can.*

* *"Everyone you know knows someone you should know." Find out who that someone is.*

CHAPTER TEN

Give Back—And Share the Success

Have you ever rappelled off the side of a building? Jim did and lived to talk about it. In June 2015, he ascended to the seventeenth floor of the Marriott hotel in Irvine, California, strapped on rappelling gear, and stepped outside onto the roof. It was windy up there, much more so than on the ground. *Oh, crap*, Jim thought. He had never done anything like this before, and he was (and is) afraid of heights. Hazarding a look over the edge, he saw the entire team from our office waving up at him, as well as several photographers and a videographer, their cameras pointed skyward. Bob, who was standing on the ground with our team, remembers a tiny head sticking over the edge of the building and the person up there offering a scared, little wave. Jim remembers offering a vigorous, manly wave. But he admits that for a terrifying moment he thought: *What the hell am I doing?*

Mountaineering experts on the roof checked Jim's gear and told him exactly what to do. One of them must have seen how nervous he was. "How you doing?" he asked in a thick, Australian accent. "You feeling okay mate?" It seemed to take a long time for Jim to get ready for his descent. Bob thought maybe Jim was having second thoughts when the scheduled time for Jim's rappel came and went.

Jim's fear dissipated as he began rappelling. His harness did all the work, and his ropes had a safety mechanism that automatically locked if he descended faster than six feet per second. Several minutes later, he was back on solid earth. Bob remembers that he had the biggest smile on his face—whether expressing relief or a sense of accomplishment, he couldn't tell. Jim was just beaming, and he continued beaming for a good half hour.

What would possess a mild-mannered guy like Jim to rappel down a building? It had to do with a tragedy that had befallen a friend of ours. In 2011 a former CEO in the hotel industry, Gary Mendell, lost his son Brian to suicide. Brian had been addicted to drugs, and the shame associated with that addiction led him to take his own life. Determined to spare others from the same fate, Mendell created a non-profit organization called "Shatterproof." Its mission is "to protect our children from addiction to alcohol or other drugs and end the stigma and suffering of those affected by this disease." Jim's high-wire act took place as part of the Shatterproof Challenge, the beginning of what will be more involvement on our part in the organization.

You've probably heard a lot about the "sharing economy." There is job sharing, or in the case of Chip Conley's company Airbnb, a shared social experience that benefits both homeowners (the business) and travelers (the customer). Let's add shared success as well. Talk of "corporate social responsibility" has buzzed around boardrooms for years, but in recent years the trend toward giving back has intensified. Just look at the phenomenon of B Corporations (or "Benefits" corporations, as they are known). These "for profit" companies commit to making a material positive impact on society and/or the environment, for the benefit of employees and the community. Most companies take as their primary responsibility increasing shareholder value. With B Corps, it's not all about profits; it's about giving back and doing good. Since 2010, when Maryland set in place the structure for a B Corporation, twenty-eight states have put these corporations in place, with more likely to follow.

By our definition, any partnership you might form should be broadly construed to include partnership with the broader community. Give, and don't expect anything in return. If the industry or community in which you work gets stronger, bigger, and better as a result of your efforts, *is that a bad thing*? Additionally, the act of doing good for a third party can help a partnership deepen and solidify, since each party comes to view the joint contributions as a source of personal inspiration, pride, and energy. The partnership becomes stronger, and better business results usually follow in turn.

YOU DON'T HAVE TO BE BILL GATES

When we first started our company, we had never heard of a B Corporation, but we did seek to actively support good causes and share any success we achieved. Although we didn't have millions to give away, we realized we could have an impact by baking a social mission right into our business model. The founding document of our main event, The Americas Lodging Investment Summit (ALIS), states that a significant portion of the event's proceeds would fund research, education, and scholarships for students interested in hospitality as a career. In structuring the event in this way, we were inspired by Ben and Jerry's, a partnership that committed a fixed percentage of profits to charity. We also looked to actor Paul Newman, who donated all the proceeds of his Newman's Own bottled salad dressing to worthy causes. Including a built-in sharing component into our business model allowed us to lock in our commitment, making it an inviolable element of our partnership. If we succeeded financially, the broader hotel community would succeed as well.

We chose education because we saw a need that we could address as well as a chance to help build our industry's future. We produced our initial big event in partnership with an industry group, The Educational Institute (EI) of the American Hotel and Lodging Association (AHLA). EI and its related foundation were specifically devoted to hospitality education and training. The Educational Institute would give our event instant legitimacy and a purpose in the industry, and we knew we could rely on them to use the money well for scholarships and academic research relating to hospitality. Like us, the EI and its parent organization, AHLA, committed in writing to use proceeds from the event in the way we all intended. A large percentage of the money we generated would go right back into the industry, helping to make it bigger, better, and more prosperous.

At the time, partnering with a non-profit when setting up a for-profit business model was quite unique. Even today, relatively few companies have relationships like this as a core part of their business. That's too bad: As of this writing, we've generated $15 million for hospitality education, training, and research—over $1 million for every year we've been in business. That's not Bill & Melinda Gates-level philanthropy, but for a niche business that started with one employee and that has grown to seven, it's not too shabby. If you build social purpose into the core of your partnership, great things can happen little by little without you even realizing it. One day you might wake up and realize that your impact has far exceeded your expectations.

We soon discovered all sorts of ways that we could use our new business to further good causes. Shortly after we started the ALIS conference, two young activists working with the local Habitat for Humanity chapter approached us. As they had realized, hotels buy new furniture and fixtures every five to seven years, and the old furnishings the hotel disposes of often still have useful lives. Together, we thought, "wouldn't it be great if the hotel could donate these items to Habitat, who could then in turn sell it to the public in stores, not unlike Goodwill Stores?" The money generated from the sale of these hotel goods would be used to build more houses. What a neat idea! The hotel would receive a tax deduction and the satisfaction of contributing to building better neighborhoods. Habitat would realize another source of income. More people in the community would get better housing. This was indeed shared success at its best.

We didn't own hotels, and we certainly didn't have much money to give to Habitat, so we couldn't help directly. What we did have, thanks to our newly formed ALIS event, was an ability to shine a spotlight on this great idea. And that's what we did. For two years in a row, we gave Habitat a slot in the event to tell hoteliers how this idea works, and we also created an auction to raise money for them. Our own business got nothing measurable out of it; on the contrary, it took a lot of time and effort to put the auction together. But we didn't mind. As we saw it, sharing success formed the basis of ALIS, and indeed of our company. If we (and our industry) could help improve communities by working with this fine organization, why not do it?

GET INVOLVED

The next time you visit the Holiday Inn at the Mumbai (India) International Airport, you might notice a slight young woman named Rosy helping you find a seat at the hotel's restaurant. Rosy had trouble with school, leaving without a high school diploma. Yet she dreamed of escaping India's rampant poverty, making a good living, and achieving financial independence. With the help of a mentor, she took part in a program called Youth Career Initiative (YCI) that helps at-risk young people in a dozen developing countries launch careers in the hospitality industry. To break the cycle of poverty that so often ensnares kids, the Initiative offers six-month internships that provide intensive skills training and helps kids build the confidence they need to make productive lives. Kids learn basic lessons in professionalism such as how to dress, how to speak, how to serve customers, and so on.

Rosy needed help building her skills, especially around communication, but administrators of her program were impressed by her "naturally charming and approachable personality" and judged that she had potential. Rosy worked hard and made strong progress. As she remembers: "Initially I had difficulties about long duty hours, dealing with guests and understanding the course content. But over a period of time, I came to like the programme and realized that I could fulfill my dream of making a career in the hospitality sector."[19] Upon finishing the program, Rosy received a job offer from Holiday Inn—a full-time position. Today she loves her work and gets along great with her colleagues; she is eager to spread the word about how YCI helps kids like her. "I would like to tell all those wishing to enroll for the YCI programme that they must take it seriously and work hard, as this is a wonderful opportunity for them to make a career in the hospitality industry."

YCI truly changes lives, and when we heard about the organization, we simply had to become involved. Because of Bob's extremely difficult childhood, he remembers craving attention from someone—*anyone*—who believed in his potential and could help him reach it. Lacking sufficient mentorship and support, he was left to flounder; it was only when he met Jim that he really put himself on a fulfilling, productive path. By that time he was already thirty years old. Today, his heart goes out to the kids in YCI, because they're in an even tougher place.

For both of us, YCI is a special cause. It helps kids, and it also helps the industry we love. The hotels that participate earn enormous good will not only from the community, but from employees who are proud to see their hotel engaged in this program. In giving back, we make sure to choose causes we can get behind not merely intellectually, but emotionally—causes that truly tug at our hearts. We try to find causes that inspire us to give *all* of ourselves (even if that involves overcoming extreme anxiety and rappelling down a tall building). Many companies are content to cut checks for charitable causes and put the bulk of their energy and attention elsewhere. We want to *be there* for our causes, not only once or twice, but over the long term. We also want to help in all kinds of ways, financial contributions being just a part of it.

As we did with Habitat for Humanity, we give YCI a platform at our events to build awareness in the industry about their mission and accomplishments. We started supporting the organization when they launched in Mumbai and then Delhi. Later, we committed support to YCI in Latin America, and most recently in Southeast Asia. We know that the financial contributions we make from the conferences help their efforts, but we think the platform we are also able to provide them is even more valuable. When we first began promoting YCI, most hotel owners had no clue that the organization existed. Today when hotel owners learn about YCI, they're eager to be a part of it. If we can encourage everyone in our industry to get involved, the impact will be far greater than anything we could do on our own. Hotel industry competitors working side by side to support this program: It's the ultimate in collaboration!

DECIDING WHOM TO HELP

We're approached all the time by charitable causes seeking financial contributions. Obviously we can't say "yes," all the time, or even most of the time. To determine if a group is a good match for our partnership, we ask ourselves a series of questions. We share these questions with you in hopes they'll help you and your partners find the most meaningful and satisfying ways of giving back.

1. Does this cause or organization resonate with us as human beings, and do we deeply understand it?

2. Can we see ourselves wanting to help this cause or organization for many years to come? Will the cause or organization be around for a while?

3. Does the cause or organization somehow relate to our business or industry?

4. Are there important ways we can help besides just giving money, and is the organization open to us being actively involved?

5. Do we *both* feel strongly about this cause or organization? And will we be able to mobilize our employees and our partners around this cause or organization?

6. Can our involvement in this cause or organization make an important difference?

7. Do we have the time or money to become involved meaningfully with this cause or organization? Realizing that our resources are limited, how does this way of giving back rank against others we might consider?

It's especially important to find causes that feel authentic to you. *The Amazing Race* co-creators Bertram van Munster and Elise Doganieri focus on helping out the local communities where the *The Amazing Race* films, and doing so in a way that allows the show's contestants to participate. Quite often, the show will support children, helping out local schools and orphanages. In Zambia, Africa, the production team brought boxes of supplies to an orphanage, with the children getting a chance to meet the contestants. On other occasions, the show has donated bicycles, tables, school chairs, and other items used on the show to local children. In Sri Lanka, *The Amazing Race* donated money to help local residents rebuild after a tsunami hit. Routinely the show builds awareness about social and environmental issues among its millions of viewers.

In order for a cause to feel authentic, it's important that it be something that *everyone* in your partnership can get behind. Having been raised Catholic, Jim might feel passionately about supporting a Catholic cause, but it may not be something Bob feels strongly about. He's not a big fan of organized religion, so we don't do it. It's our *combined* interests that count. For this reason, it's important to begin posing these questions early on in your partnership, maybe even before you formally sign on as partners. If you can't find common ground about causes to support, that might suggest a more fundamental lack of compatibility.

We've realized over time that we have a "sweet spot" where getting involved is concerned. We tend to agree on causes that help out kids in need, that have some kind of educational component, and ideally, that also help our industry. Shatterproof fits those criteria: its founder was an important figure in our industry, and the organization dedicates itself to helping kids suffering from addiction. YCI likewise is a bull's-eye. Kids (check!), education (check!), hotels (check!). The hotel industry educational institute and foundation—kids (check!), education (check!), hotels (check!). In recent years, we've helped support a program in New York City, You Gotta Believe, which helps older foster kids who have little hope of finding "forever" families. Since we've been branching into the entertainment industry, we've begun helping organizations in that area, such as the Actor's Fund, which provides assistance and social services for actors and entertainment professionals in need. Just like we've invested ourselves in hospitality, now we want to do our part to help the entertainment industry grow and succeed.

GIVING BACK— IT'S NOT JUST FOR BHBS

Are we hopeless romantics or BHBs (bleeding heart business-people)? Yes and yes. But even if you and your partners are not, sharing and giving back is still great to do. We've always believed that if we imbued our business with a greater purpose, the business would do just fine, and even if it didn't, then at least we will have done some good along the way. In fact, we believe that giving back has contributed to our own financial success more than any other principle described in this book. We say "believe" because we can't document a direct link between our social cause-related activity and our business results. Yet we don't need such documentation—the link is intuitive and obvious.

Josh Kilmer-Purcell and his life and business partner Brent Ridge, television's Fabulous Beekman Boys and founders of the small-farm lifestyle brand and website Beekman 1802, also appreciate the business benefits of giving back. When they wanted to donate a portion of the proceeds of their branded tomato sauce, they immediately settled on a cause: Helping small farm entrepreneurs who are trying to build businesses. As Brent explains, this cause felt deeply personal to both of them. "We knew how hard it was for us starting a farm-based business and how almost impossible it is to get out from under the mortgage and the capital expenses of all the equipment and whatnot." It also felt authentic to the spirit of their business.

From the very beginning, the two focused on creating a business that would benefit small producers in their own Upstate New York farming village, either by employing them directly or by giving them a way to market their products through the Beekman's website. The very existence of their business helped the community by enabling it to prevent its own small post office, the hub of community life, from closing!

As Josh noted, their charitable program is as much an indirect investment for them as it is a charitable donation. By finding and funding entrepreneurs who were "doing interesting and innovative things," the two were helping nurture a network of individuals whom they might one day be able to engage as business partners. "We look at what they're doing. We're like, "That's amazing. At some point, we're going to find a way to use that, so we need to help you grow it," and so we invest money in what they're doing, not expecting anything back. If it eventually makes sense to work together, we know that the money we put in will come back to us."

As of this writing, that money is coming back to them, in ways and to an extent the Beekmans could never have imagined. The tomato sauce and its charitable purpose resonated with consumers. The retailing giant Target noticed and approached the Beekmans with a proposition: Would they be willing to develop an entire line of products especially for Target stores that likewise conveyed the philosophy of supporting small farms? Uh, can you say *yes!* In November 2015, just two years after launching their tomato sauce, Kilmer-Purcell and Ridge had a whole section of their products available in Target's grocery section, including salsa, baking products, condiments, and salad dressing, all created in collaboration with small farms and manufacturers.

The lesson is clear: Every time you do something for your industry, you're also building goodwill. In our case, we know that our customers care about our industry's fortunes, and that they respect us for supporting hospitality education. Our commitment distinguishes us from many of our competitors, making our customers more loyal. They like our product, but they also feel a little better about spending money on it. Also, because part of our profits support educational ventures, we're helping to establish our brand with a rising generation of potential customers. The kids we help will be tomorrow's hospitality executives, responsible for determining which investment conferences they'll attend. If they remember our company as the one that helped them build their careers, chances are they'll attend our conferences.

Even greater than these benefits are the *internal* ones the partnership will reap. As corny as it sounds, we get an amazing feeling from knowing we've made a difference. When we look into the eyes of a young person who says, "Thank you for helping me," it impacts us profoundly. Our partnership benefits because we have the chance to work towards a common goal, above and beyond the obvious one of building a thriving business and making money. Achieving financial success is great, but we have the sense that we're building something positive and leaving a legacy. It drives us to work even harder to sustain and grow our business, and it makes our employees want to work harder and give more of themselves. All of us are simply a little prouder of what we do, knowing that we've done our little part to make the world a better place.

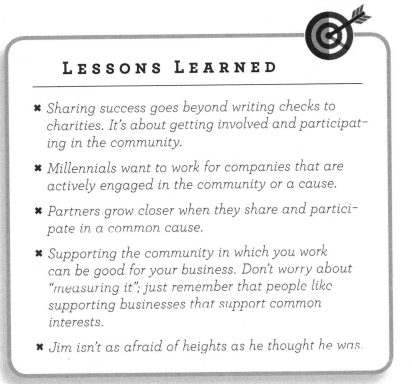

LESSONS LEARNED

* *Sharing success goes beyond writing checks to charities. It's about getting involved and participating in the community.*

* *Millennials want to work for companies that are actively engaged in the community or a cause.*

* *Partners grow closer when they share and participate in a common cause.*

* *Supporting the community in which you work can be good for your business. Don't worry about "measuring it"; just remember that people like supporting businesses that support common interests.*

* *Jim isn't as afraid of heights as he thought he was.*

CHAPTER ELEVEN

Don't Slip Off the Balance Beam

Iconic lyricist and Academy Award-winner Johnny Mercer wrote the words to classic songs like "Moon River," "Hooray for Hollywood," and "On the Atchison, Topeka, and the Santa Fe" (the last of these sung by our pal Lorna Luft's mom, Judy Garland, in the film *The Harvey Girls*). We have a special connection to Johnny, since as we've mentioned, we own his former home in Palm Springs. We love his songs, but our favorite Mercer tune is: "Ac-Cent-Tchu-Ate the Positive." Our favorite part of that song is: "You've got to Accentuate the positive/ Eliminate the negative/Latch on to the affirmative/Don't mess with Mister In-Between."

We live by these words. Negativity has a way of easily seeping in and taking control of people's lives, so we continually remind ourselves to "accentuate the positive." We don't ignore reality. We've had our share of bad stuff happen, but we know that if we re-adjust our thinking to focus on the good things, life becomes easier. Bob likes to say (yes, another Bobism), "Good things come out of bad situations." The key is to maintain a healthy balance between positive and negative (without feeling like we're stuck "messing with Mister In-Between").

Balance in general is essential to keeping personal and business relationships on track as they mature. "Life is about balance," Ellen DeGeneres said in her book *Seriously . . . I'm Kidding*. "The good and the bad. The highs and the lows. The piña and the colada." In partnerships, a lack of balance can create incredible stress or worse. When one partner consistently takes on too much work, for instance, the other might lose interest or become resentful. A downward spiral can ensue, leading to the partnership's eventual unraveling.

Strong partnerships require that each partner also retain a sense of balance internally, maintaining autonomy and a life beyond the partnership. It's important that each partner make time for family, friends, and hobbies, even though this has become infinitely harder to manage in our age of constant digital communication. Here again, we must attend to the "me" if the "we" is to work.

Balance might look differently for different partnerships; an arrangement that works in one instance might not work in another. Yet one thing is certain: Balance of any kind is never easy—it requires constant care, attention, and commitment from all parties. Even the best partnerships get off kilter at times. But if you take a disciplined approach, accentuating the positive when you need to, picking up the slack when your partner hasn't contributed enough, and keeping communication open at all times, you can push through the tough times, sustain a healthy tension and enhance your prospects for long term growth and success.

THE POWER OF SEVEN

Balancing between work and family becomes especially vexing when business partners are also romantically involved (like us!) or are family members. If you live with your business partner, how do you stop yourselves from talking business 24/7 or from letting your personal issues burst out in every company meeting? As Ivanka Trump told us, she's found that a family business is "either a tremendous success or a terrible failure. You don't often hear about family members working together and having an "okay" relationship. It's very polarized." Trump considers herself fortunate that she, her father, and her brothers genuinely love and respect one another and thus are able to generally stay in balance. "Our family works together day in and day out, and while it's not effortless, we have a very tight bond and a great dynamic. We're all incredibly hard working. Strife can occur in a family business—or, frankly, any partnership—when one person bears the burden of the work necessary to make their project, task or relationship a success. That simply doesn't happen with our family."[20]

We became business partners precisely because Jim was having trouble finding balance in his own life between work and home. As we've mentioned, for the first ten years of our relationship, there was a third presence in our home: Jim's job. At first, Bob tried to live with the imbalance, thinking that Jim would change and the relationship would balance out over time. Big mistake—you should never enter a partnership hoping your partner will change into what you want them to be. Bob would pester Jim to save room for personal time. Jim resisted, and we would bicker over it. As time passed, Bob became increasingly annoyed at how little time Jim had for "us."

A turning point came several years into our relationship when we were supposed to take a week's vacation in London. Bob was about to start a new job, so this was his last opportunity to vacation for a while. Several days before the trip, he reminded Jim to allow time for packing. "Sure, okay," Jim said. Two days before takeoff, Bob checked in on Jim's suitcase status. Still nothing. "Yeah, yeah, I'm on top of it."

The night before we were supposed to leave, Jim still wasn't packed. "What's going on? Why aren't you packed?" Bob asked.

A sheepish look came over Jim's face. "I can't go."

"What do you mean you can't go?"

"I just can't. I have too much going on at work."

We didn't go on that trip, and Bob was more than a little annoyed—it was the closest he has ever been to breaking up with Jim. He realized then that Jim was never going to change, Jim's work was going to be a priority, and that it was time to make a decision. Would Bob continue to fight? Did he have any hope of winning out over Jim's job? Concluding that he didn't, Bob started thinking that perhaps a solution—albeit a radical one—was to join forces with Jim professionally. This was risky for all kinds of reasons, but Bob felt it might be riskier still to not make the move. Bob did make the move, and happily, it more than worked out. With Bob helping out, Jim found it easier to take more time off.

Of course, becoming business partners while also romantic partners meant that we had to take steps to prevent our work from overwhelming all else. Bob would come home from work at 6 p.m. and turn on the television or pick up a book, winding down for the day and thinking about anything but business. Around seven or eight, Jim would come home all wound up and wanting to talk business. Something similar happened in the morning: Jim would get up as early as 5 a.m. and wait for Bob to wake up so he could share a business idea that had come to him overnight. As soon as Bob stirred, Jim pounced, throwing numbers at him while Bob's brain was still hazy with sleep. Bob hadn't even had his first caffeine fix most of the time.

Realizing that this routine couldn't last, we instituted what we call our Seven-Seven Rule. No talking business before seven o'clock in the morning or after seven o'clock at night. That's not to say Jim can't think about business—he can, and he can put his ideas for Bob into an email that Bob can read later at his leisure. But no *talking* business for twelve hours per day. This rule works. We both live by it, only making an exception if we both agree to break the rule. Guess who usually wants to break the rule and guess who usually wants to invoke it? Some things never change . . .

THE POWER OF EIGHTS?

We've spoken to others who have family members as partners, and many have versions of this Seven-Seven Rule. Trina Turk and Jonathan Skow have an "eight o'clock" rule—or at least Jonathan does. "I have trouble sometimes falling asleep if I'm pissed, so I don't like to talk about things at night that are annoying. Not just 'big-annoying'—the little things, like HR matters. Trina is always bringing stuff up, and I'm like, It's after eight, I don't want to talk about this!'"[21]

Jonathan Tisch, who runs the Loews Corporation with his cousins Jim and Andrew, told us that the three of them sometimes discuss business at family gatherings, but they never take it *too* far. "We respect each other's family time. We respect when we are with our significant others, when I'm with my wife and kids. We're all in our 60s now, [so we have an] understanding of what works in terms of business, and what works in terms of family time."[22]

Family businesses meld personal and professional life—you just have to accept that. While it's important to have boundaries in place, you also have to keep these boundaries somewhat fluid, intuitive, and open to change. Gavin Newsom (as of 2015, the Lieutenant Governor of California) is part owner of PlumpJack Hospitality Group with his sister Hilary, and they do talk business at family events. "One of the great things about starting a business," he told us, "is how it weaves into your life naturally and isn't 'work.' I always enjoyed using those off-moments that weren't 'work related'—Thanksgiving celebrations, or birthdays—to have conversations about the business. But these were always benign or easy conversations. We didn't have conversations about, say, accounting. Any attempt to do that always ended very badly."

Hilary added that although the conversations didn't touch on accounting, they often did lead to vibrant brainstorming about new ideas for the business: "We're all talking about experiences we've had, restaurants we've eaten at, really good recipe ideas—those are the moments when you can actually dedicate the time [to think] because it's not forced. There's no time limit, no one-hour meeting. You're just having these free-flowing conversations about really interesting experiences, and we can borrow from those and integrate them into our business. These are actually some of the most creative times for our family."[23]

As wonderful as these kinds of encounters sound, most members of a family partnership still need time when they are *completely* off duty—either alone or together. Trina and Jonathan confided that they found it hard to ever truly "get away" from work (we hear them on that one!). Yet as their business has grown and they've spent more time together running it, Jonathan has made more of an effort to break off during the week and do his own thing. In his case, that often involves swimming, a pastime that has also afforded him his own set of non-work friends. The Beekman Boys told us that while they both find themselves almost constantly working, they are still able to spend valuable time away from one another; the farm on which they live and run their business is so large that they can spend entire days working apart, only meeting up again at dinner time. Elise Doganieri and her life and business partner Bertram van Munster will sometimes drive separately to work even if they have the same schedule, solely for the purpose of getting some alone time.

In our case, Jim travels a lot for work, which gives Bob enough alone time. When we're together, we make a point of socializing with nonbusiness related friends and taking frequent trips to our vacation home in Palm Springs. This gives us much-needed psychological distance from work.

BALANCE AND DECISION MAKING

Maintaining balance isn't just about downshifting the business talk at times; it's about making an array of decisions with balance in mind. We consciously set up our business so that we can manage the workflow without killing one another and ourselves. We spread out the events we produce throughout the year, allowing for some down times during which we can take a few days off to catch up with friends or just do nothing. We take these mini-breaks as much as possible (but in the spirit of full disclosure we haven't done a good job taking the one, two, or heaven forbid, three-week vacation). All year long as we gaze at our calendars, we're talking with one another about how to maintain balance. We ask ourselves: Is what we're taking on realistic? Are we scheduling ourselves too tightly? What do each of us need in terms of down time and romantic time with one another?

We especially consider balance when deciding whether or not to jump in on new business opportunities. A given opportunity that comes our way might sound amazing on its merits, but it doesn't work in the broader context of our existing commitments. We've unfortunately passed up great opportunities because when we looked at all the competing demands on our resources, we felt we wouldn't be able to strike a reasonable or sustainable balance. In one instance, a friend of ours approached us about buying out a small but profitable set of businesses he had built. He ran events very similar to the ones we put on, only elsewhere in the world. We thought we could easily merge his business with ours, helping us grow. In just one deal, we'd increase the size of our business by almost 50 percent. Jim, the visionary among us, was frothing at the mouth.

Just as we were about to make an offer, the "Mr. No" among us, Bob, started asking questions about whether we could handle the deal. Did we mention that the company was headquartered in a foreign country, a long plane ride and many time zones from our home? How would we manage the employees and handle other company logistics? On top of that, we'd have to learn all the nuances of running a company in this foreign country—the tax codes, the laws around human resources, and so on. None of this was impossible, but was it really the right time for us to be taking it on?

We were then in the midst of searching for a new operations manager, but we hadn't yet found that person. If we had, the analysis might have been different, but as it stood, Jim would have had to shoulder much of the burden of running the new company. Our time was already maxed out; we had to hire an analyst because we didn't even have time to understand basic things about the new business. If we proceeded, the extra time required would probably have come from our already limited personal time. Much as we wanted to pull the trigger on the deal, we passed.

Today Jim will admit that we made the right call. Taking over another company is a serious endeavor, and you have to be sure you can commit without throwing yourself off balance and putting too much pressure on your existing commitments. Whenever we consider expanding our business, we try to *over-estimate* the resources that might be required. That way, we're protecting our existing businesses, and we can feel pleasantly surprised when the expansion doesn't turn out to be as time-consuming or costly as we thought.

On a number of occasions, we've assessed how prospective deals would affect balance in our partnership and said an enthusiastic *yes*. Our decision to enter the film business, for instance, might have seemed foolhardy. With a demanding schedule of events to produce, how could we enter moviemaking (about which we knew very little) and still get everything done? But we knew we could. Going "all in" to produce our first film entailed a financial investment, but a relatively small investment of time. What time we did spend was limited to the few months when the film was actually in postproduction. After that, we could sit back, cross our fingers, and hopefully count our royalty checks.

Our decision to write this book reflected a similar thought process. We knew we'd need to devote significant time to it, but only for several months. As we looked at the opportunity, we realized that we could finish the book during a lull in our events schedule and before work on our next movie ramped up, all without reducing our personal time together unduly. In fact, the book project brought the two of us together for periods of time and allowed us to talk about things other than the business. We were able to reflect back on our lives together for the past twenty-five years, something we seldom do on our own. It was fun to relive a lot of the ups and downs of our relationship. As Jim said to Bob, "I learned a lot about you through this process."

When considering opportunities, it's also important to consider our external partners and how they are balancing their own commitments. We produce many of our events in partnership with others, and in many cases, they have multiple businesses or other projects on their plate. While we typically come up with the new ideas in a partnership, we always reach a consensus before proceeding and only after talking about any increased demands on everyone's time. The network of relationships underpinning any successful business is large and complicated, and these relationships need to work well together. When they don't and the balance gets upset—that's when you run into trouble.

REBALANCING

Even with the most kind, sensitive, thoughtful, and self-reflective partners, it's still easy to lose control and veer off track. What then?

We try to respond quickly to a potential imbalance by staying alert to the warning signs. If one of our partners is failing to respond to phone calls, it may signal that he or she is overburdened, unhappy, and pulling back, or it may mean nothing at all about the business. We try to pay attention to subtle shifts in our relationships—small, daily habits that have gone by the wayside, a feeling that things have just felt "off" lately in our business, a sense that our partner is distracted and unable to focus. These could suggest that our partner is experiencing personal difficulties (health, financial, relationship, or otherwise) that make him less able to fulfill his obligations.

Once we detect a true imbalance, we determine what's behind it. It may be that something has happened in our partner's life that has diverted her attention but that will be resolved quickly. She might have suffered a death in her family, for instance, and after the mourning period, her performance will return to normal. Or it might be that our partner has certain goals in her personal life that she is working to achieve, and once they are, she can return her focus to business.

After Hilary and Gavin Newsom had been partnering for some time, Hilary became aware that PlumpJack had become her entire life—she was eating, sleeping, breathing the business.

She hadn't minded this so far; she loved that her brother was calling her at any time of day and on weekends to talk about work, and she felt that the business had given her "all the good things in life." Yet after a while, she wanted to settle down and get married, and she needed more time away from work to develop her romantic life. In particular, she wanted to date a man she'd met who lived in Los Angeles, a day's drive from her house. What had once seemed an appropriate balance for her now seemed to be an imbalance—and a permanent one at that, unless she and Gavin could negotiate a change.

That's precisely what they did. One Saturday, Gavin called her in the afternoon, asking her to meet to talk about a business issue. "I can't," she said, "I'm out of town."

"What?"

"Yeah, I'm dating someone and can't work weekends anymore."

As Hilary recalls, her brother was stunned—he hadn't considered that she would need more time to herself. Yet he understood and acceded to Hilary's need for a bit more distance. Good thing: Hilary wound up marrying her boyfriend. Her need for more personal time to travel to LA proved temporary, as her husband moved up to Northern California to live with her. Hilary was able to meet with Gavin on weekends once again. Today, Hilary respects the needs of her own employees for balance in their lives, both on a temporary and permanent basis. "When I interview people, I tell them, 'This is a lifestyle company. I will never demand more of you than you want to give, and I want you to have a life.'" She finds that the best employees are those who can go off into their personal lives and then come back with both energy and ideas to drive the business further.[24]

In some cases, the underlying cause of an imbalance might require more significant adjustments. As we've seen, Trina and

Jonathan noticed that they were working hard to grow their business, while their initial partner wasn't. Probing that imbalance, they discovered that their partner had very different goals for the business than theirs. She would fight any attempt to grow it, which meant that Trina and Jonathan either had to agree to keep the business small or else find a way to phase out their partner. We've seen similar dynamics play out in romantic relationships. In a married couple we know, one partner was much more dominant and controlling than the other. The more subservient partner eventually got sick of this imbalance and tried to rectify it by behaving more assertively. When the dominant one couldn't handle this change, the relationship declined and the two eventually divorced.

If the causes of an imbalance are deeper or more permanent, try to see if you can adjust the relationship in ways acceptable both to you and your partner. When confronted with his partner's mental illness, Tom Corcoran decided that he was willing to accept a new arrangement—a redefined balance or status quo—in which his partner was absent for long periods of time, and he took on the burden of running the company. We've done something similar when our own partners have underperformed. We haven't always been happy about taking on extra work, but in those cases we ultimately concluded that we stood to lose more if the partnerships fell apart.

GROWING TOGETHER

If you stick with a partnership as long as we have, you realize that the real benefit of balance isn't just an enduring relationship; it's a relationship that enables ongoing growth and synergy. In business and in romance, nothing feels worse than a stagnant relationship. And when a relationship is stuck, often the individuals in the relationship are stuck as well. By constantly working to keep our relationship in balance, focusing on our business enough to satisfy Jim but still leaving enough time for a personal life together to satisfy Bob, we have allowed ourselves to grow and change over time.

Jim today still focuses mainly on work—he loves it as much as ever. Bob still has to drag him away from his desk some nights. But as Bob will grudgingly admit, this challenge has gotten easier over the years: Jim appreciates the virtues of time away much more than he used to, and to Bob's delight, he'll sometimes *initiate* time off on his own. "We've been working hard," Jim will say. "Let's get away and just do nothing for a couple of days." Jim had a recent milestone birthday and we went to Italy and Lake Como for a week. To Bob's pleasant surprise, he left his cell phone at home! Jim was antsy at first, but he rediscovered what life was like before email, and he liked it. With time and effort, people can change, or at least soften around their edges.

Meanwhile, the ongoing process of sustaining balance leads to a deepening respect between partners over time. Hopefully, the parties to any partnership respect one another from the outset, but as time passes and they discover that their partners accept them even while challenging them to grow and adapt, they naturally come to respect one another even more. "I go back to the word 'respect,'" Jonathan Tisch remarked. "Respect what people want in their lives. It might be different than what you want in your life. In our family, we learned to cut each other slack, to allow one another to be individuals and pursue goals in life that are important to us not only in terms of work."[25]

We wholeheartedly agree. One reason we've been together so long is that while Jim's workaholism drove Bob crazy, and Bob's social needs drove Jim crazy, we each respected our differences along the way. We were willing to work with the other person, pushing hard at times when we thought the balance had been skewed, but not pushing too hard as to prevent the other from being himself.

SCORING A TOUCHDOWN

The Loews Corporation is a multibillion dollar goliath today, but as Jonathan Tisch recounted, its roots were extraordinarily humble. In 1946, his father and uncle took over as operators of a summer camp in Lakewood, New Jersey. Two years later, they heard that the big hotel in town, Laurel-in-the-Pines, was available for lease. They didn't know much about hospitality, but they hadn't known about running a summer camp, and they'd succeeded in that. Thus began a business expansion that continues to this day, extending to hotels, insurance, offshore drilling and natural gas pipelines. Oh, and sports: In 1991, Jonathan's late father Bob purchased a 50 percent stake in the New York Giants pro football team that today is owned by Jon, his brother Steve and his sister Laurie.

This success story is in part about balance and the great potential unleashed when partners can sustain a nice equilibrium over time. In the case of Jonathan's father Bob and Uncle Larry, that equilibrium entailed a balance between Bob's people skills and Larry's analytical skills. "Bob was known as 'Mr. Outside.' He would walk into a hotel and know the names of all the employees and where their kids went to college. He said hello to everyone. Larry, 'Mr. Inside,' was a financial wizard in an era before private equity and hedge funds. It was the combination of the two that allowed our family to grow Loews Corporation into what it is today." A similar equilibrium also took root with the New York Giants, which the Tisch family operates in partnership with the Mara family. "It was a partnership that [my father] was willing to work at. They each brought very different skills to the table. Each had his roles and responsibilities. Each understood the other's point of view. Here we are today, still partners with the Mara family, and it has been very successful."[26]

Balance and the respect that underlies it is the recipe not just for success, but for enduring success, even a *legacy* of success. Pick up a newspaper on any given day, and you'll read about business and romantic relationships that have tanked because the parties couldn't sustain balance between them, or because the parties couldn't balance the demands of their partnership with other parts of their lives. Balance is hard work indeed, and in this era of narcissism, greed, and distraction, it often seems as if both the grit and underlying respect necessary for enduring partnerships is in short supply. If you find a quality partner, pay close attention to his or her needs, working hard to keep your partnership balanced and a productive tension intact. Pay attention to boundaries, clearly defining them yet keeping them sufficiently porous. Discover, over time, your own definition of balance. Bring out the best in one another, and accept the worst. Years later, when you look back on what you've accomplished, you'll find that you really did score a touchdown.

LESSONS LEARNED

* *Balance is one of the most difficult aspects of partnership, requiring a concerted effort on the part of each partner to maintain.*

* *An unbalanced personal life can lead to an unbalanced business partnership.*

* *Balance doesn't necessarily mean a 50/50 split in roles, but it does mean that the partners' responsibilities break down in a reasonable way. Maintaining balance in a partnership starts with respecting each partner's unique qualities, desires, and needs.*

* *People who partner with the same person in life and business have to work particularly hard at balancing their relationship. Sustaining outside interests is important and we strongly recommend the 7/7 rule.*

CHAPTER TWELVE

Change the Sheets

One morning in August 2015, we were sitting in our kitchen in Palm Springs, enjoying coffee together and chatting about work (it was three minutes past seven), when Jim pointed to his laptop screen. "Bob, they're doing it! They're changing the sheets."

"Changing the sheets?" Bob wasn't sure what Jim was talking about—it was still early in the morning for him.

Jim turned his laptop around so Bob could see the website of the *Los Angeles Times*. "Read the story about Google becoming Alphabet."

Bob skimmed the story. "Wow, they *are* changing the sheets."

Google had just announced that it was restructuring by creating a parent company for itself and its many businesses called Alphabet. All of these businesses would operate independently—each with its own leadership—under the parent company's umbrella. What we found interesting was that Google cofounder Larry Page, now Alphabet's CEO, had explicitly justified the structure as a means of injecting new energy into the business: "We've long believed that over time companies tend to get comfortable doing the same thing, just making incremental changes. But in the technology industry, where revolutionary ideas drive the next big growth areas, you need to be a bit uncomfortable to stay relevant."[27] In the hospitality industry, we have our own term for staying a bit uncomfortable and keeping things fresh: "changing the sheets."

Changing the sheets is as important for partnerships as it is for large organizations. It's a way partners can stay innovative, engaged, energized, and just plain happy. If you don't take steps to keep yourself at least a little uncomfortable, you can become complacent, which leads in fairly short order to boredom, stagnation, decline—and we *all* know what happens after decline. Changing things up periodically is also a way partners can stay aligned over the long term. Circumstances change, and so do partners' goals and desires. Unless partners are willing to stay flexible and make changes to accommodate each other's growth and evolution, conflict can fester and ultimately destroy the relationship.

One reason we're still together, and still business partners after more than fifteen years, is because we've not only embraced change when necessary; we've pushed ourselves all along to question what we do, even revisiting the basic premise of our businesses and our relationship. We've made some significant changes on some occasions and at others merely tweaked the edges. But by constantly opening ourselves to change, we've felt consistently re-energized and recommitted, and our businesses have (so far) remained relevant and fresh.

What about you? Is your daily routine starting to get a little boring? Are you not having as much fun as you used to? Have you become aware of a lingering resentment you feel toward your partner? Has your business performance plateaued while your competitors' performance has improved? If so, you might be resting on your laurels and getting too comfortable. Don't panic. Before malaise becomes entrenched, before the air in the room gets truly stale, before you can't stand to be with your partner for another minute—for heaven's sake, change the sheets!

GUNNING FOR GROWTH

Restructuring was expected to help freshen Google's business in a number of ways. Leaders at Alphabet's constituent companies could now focus more on their specific businesses, and the performance of each business would stand out more clearly for accounting purposes. By moving Google's top layer of management to leadership roles at Alphabet, the company would have a chance to promote star talent in its ranks that might have otherwise left to pursue other opportunities.

Restructuring is hardly the only way to keep a business or partnership energized and vital. Another is branching out into entirely new products or businesses. In our case, working with Hollywood actors, directors, and writers has proven a huge boon to our own professional and personal partnership, making it fresher and more fun. For instance, we jetted over to Scotland to film a teaser for a possible new reality TV show—what an adventure that was! And this book has been an adventure as well, pushing us to open up about our lives far more than we've ever felt comfortable doing. As we told our editor, we felt like we were in therapy together for the several months we spent drafting the book. We learned how to communicate a bit more openly about some of the issues we've written about.

If starting entirely new business lines is unrealistic, don't worry: You can also inject energy into your partnership by looking to grow existing businesses that might be feeling a little stale. ALIS, our very first annual event, has also been one of our most successful. Year after year, it has attracted more attendees and made money than any other; as of 2015, it was the biggest event of its kind in the world. In part, that's because "changing the sheets" is built into the event itself. Every year, we convene participants to reimagine the event, and everything is fair game. Theoretically, we could have a *completely* different event year to year. This structure has allowed the content and format of the event to remain relevant as our industry has evolved.

Despite that dynamism, by about 2010—almost a decade after we'd started ALIS—we sensed that the event was becoming a little too routine. Or maybe it was just we who were growing complacent. The content might change, but the planning process was the same thing year after year. We resolved to up the ante. Realizing that our customers enjoyed the face time built into the event's spring planning sessions, but that they wouldn't have a chance to see one another again until the ALIS conference itself (which is held in January), we introduced a series of summer networking events held in cities across the country. These were more relaxed affairs, cocktail parties really, featuring opportunities to schmooze as well as a program of speakers talking about industry trends. Our customers loved them. In 2015, over 500 people registered to attend. Separately, we introduced a new extension of ALIS called ALIS Law, a conference within a conference that focused specifically on legal issues of interest to hotel owners and operators, such as data security, labor law, and the economic impacts of government policy. In 2016, we introduced ALIS Tech, which focuses on technology issues relevant to the hotel industry.

The new parts of the conference were fun to work on—we found ourselves loving ALIS even more. So we asked ourselves: Were there opportunities to take our other successful events even further? Turning our gaze across the Pacific, we realized that a big, ALIS-like event we do in Hong Kong was getting a little too routine, our partnership in a bit of a rut. The event was extremely successful and profitable, but again, we weren't as jazzed about it as we used to be. We were no longer tapping into the ideas brought forth from the conference's external partners to make the event bigger, stronger, and more profitable. The solution, which our partners agreed with, was expansion. We added two new events in Asia, one in Japan and the other in Singapore. The Japan event didn't work out, but the one in Singapore proved so successful that we added a second conference there. More importantly, our relationship with our external partners took on new life. We were having fun and getting together more to throw around new ideas.

TIME FOR A ROLE REVAMP?

If you're a regular attendee of ALIS, you would have noticed something a little different at our 2011 event. Ever since we started our company in 2001, Jim has been the public persona at all of our events. He's up there on stage, welcoming attendees and introducing celebrities. As a result, he's become a familiar face to many in the industry. In 2011, Bob came onstage to introduce one of our featured speakers, California Lieutenant Governor Gavin Newsom. Jim was there, too—we performed a little comedy skit together—but he was primarily arm candy for Bob.

Why the shift? Bob came out of the shadows because he felt we needed to shake up our partnership roles. Initially Bob wanted to work exclusively behind the scenes, but as time passed, he became more invested not just in our business, but in our industry as a whole. He was proud of our company and his involvement in it. He started thinking: *Why should Jim get all the glory?* It was time for him to come out of the professional "closet" he'd created for himself. It was time to emerge as the cofounder of the business.

Jim likes the idea of adjusting partnership roles periodically. He saw Bob's emergence as an important expression of our "change the sheets" principle, and he certainly had no desire to keep Bob in a closet of any kind. But we had a long-standing rule at our events that only one person from a company could be on stage at a time. With both of us onstage, we were violating that rule, perhaps opening the door to many others who would want to share the stage on a panel with their colleagues. It felt a bit self-serving to Jim to perform the skit together, a violation of our "Play it Straight" principle. Yet he relented, and we bent the rule for the sake of keeping our partnership fresh. Good thing: Bob loved being on stage and he was quite good at it. Since then, he's appeared on stage several times at our events, becoming a recognizable part of our company's public image.

This might seem like a relatively minor adjustment, and perhaps it was. Yet more change was taking place inside our company. Although our employees had always known that the two of us were co-owners of the company, they had seen Jim as "the boss." As the president of our company, he was the one who formally supervised our team, doing the hiring and the firing, and interfacing with the employees on important matters. The two of us would talk through important issues in private and make decisions together, but our employees didn't know that. For years, this arrangement worked for us, but in 2012, as part of Bob's ongoing professional renaissance (some might call it a mid-life crisis), he suggested a change that would help things work more smoothly. Instead of Jim wielding all the public authority, Bob would oversee directly areas of the company he already managed behind the scenes. Jim agreed, and we performed a little internal restructuring. Bob took formal responsibility for the administrative functions of our business, including accounting, human resources, marketing, IT and most of the facility operations, while Jim focused on customer relations, conference programming, and the hosting of our events.

This shift in our roles has injected new life into our partnership. Jim is happier because Bob has taken responsibility off his plate. Instead of managing seven employees directly, Jim now only manages four, which translates into fewer meetings, fewer performance reviews, and fewer coaching sessions. Likewise, when we make unpopular decisions, Jim no longer bears the full burden of communicating them to our team. Meanwhile, Bob has felt much more engaged and connected to our company. He feels more empowered to effect change, and when employees come to him to resolve conflicts and challenges, he also feels more needed and helpful. To boot, when the two of us are at social business events, Bob no longer feels like some mysterious person in the background. He is now known as the cofounder of BHN, and the title "Vice President" makes introductions much less awkward.

Sometimes changing the sheets is as simple as changing roles and responsibilities, while keeping operations more or less the same.

BANISH THE F-WORD

No, not *that* f-word. We're talking about fear. One of the main reasons people don't proactively change the sheets is that they're afraid of change and the unknown. It feels scary to alter a formula that's already working. You might screw something up—and for what? Better to keep things the same, right?

Wrong. It's not better. It's worse. No success is permanent. To pre-empt the inevitable downhill slide, you have to keep pushing, experimenting, making mistakes, learning from mistakes, and improving how you operate. If you do those things, you'll wind up with a dynamic business that stays in tune with the times. You'll transform yourself from a one-hit wonder into a survivor to (over time) a venerable player in your industry. As we like to say, "don't fear failure, embrace it."

The Newsom clan appreciates how deadly the fear of change can be, so they've come up with a pretty cool tactic: an annual award for the biggest failure in their company. It started when a night clerk at one of PlumpJack's hotels tried to figure out how to get rid of mosquitos that were bothering the guests. The mosquitos had infested a pond adjacent to the hotel, and a clerk seemed to think that having catfish in the water would help, since catfish eat mosquitos. Taking the initiative, he brought in some catfish and stocked the pond with them. But he hadn't factored in that raccoons like to eat catfish. A half dozen raccoons got to the fish and ran all over the hotel grounds, surprising guests and leaving half-eaten fish carcasses in their wake. Not just a few—*dozens* of carcasses. You can only imagine the sight and the smell.

After the staff cleaned up the mess, Gavin and Hilary gave him a $500 bonus and promoted him. Yes, the clerk's idea was harebrained, but at least he'd seen a problem, thought of a possible solution, and taken action to implement it. As Gavin explained, "We don't merely want to encourage risk-taking—we want to reward it. The failure award is a way of expressing to folks that you have agency, that no matter where you are in the company, you're not a bystander and you *have* a voice. We want you to share it even if you do it in the wrong way. This keeps people fresh and motivated. They're not scared of saying the wrong thing or making the wrong decision."

The competition for biggest screw-up isn't exclusively open to employees, but to management as well—even the founder. That's right: Gavin himself has won the award (although we didn't have the heart to ask him what garnered him the honor).

Can you imagine your own boss giving himself an award for something stupid he'd done? What an inspiring and liberating message that must send. Gavin and Hilary are quick to point out that employee risks must be reasonable and not reckless. It was risky for PlumpJack to market the premium cabernet its winery produced in a bottle with a screw cap, but it wasn't reckless. It's important for employees to know the difference and to see their leaders taking appropriate risks themselves. "Only if you're willing to take risks will you keep things fresh," Gavin said. "Employees have to see people in charge pushing the boundaries in responsible ways, and they have to feel that line employees, too, can take risks and effect change in the organization. When they do, they'll feel that they can grow personally and professionally, and the larger organization will thrive."[28]

Beyond their general aversion to risk-taking, we think many people hold themselves back because they're afraid to withdraw from parts of their jobs they've long performed. We know a thing or two about that: As "Type A" personalities, we both like to be in control of everything, and we get nervous at the thought of giving up control. To really embrace the "change the sheets" principle, though, it's important to become comfortable delegating tasks to others as a business grows. That's what Bob did in 2013, when Jim proposed hiring someone else to handle our mundane bookkeeping tasks. Having performed these tasks for fifteen years, Bob was getting bored with them—*really* bored—but he still felt uncomfortable having someone else sign our checks and track our expenses. He was used to reconciling our accounts to the penny and to paying our bills the very moment they came in—what employee could be so thorough? Yet at Jim's urging, Bob finally agreed to hire someone, and he's glad he did. Not only does he have more time for more interesting work, like writing this book, but he also has more brain space to think creatively about all aspects of our business.

Bill Marriott, Sr. said it well: "Don't do anything someone else can do for you."[29] The sentiment is right on, but to put it into practice, you have to overcome your irrational fears that someone else *can't* do things as well as you can. Usually, they can. Sometimes, they can do it even better.

None of this is to say that you should change *too* much about your partnership or anything else in your business. We have a colleague in our industry that, over a period of several years, changed his events *way* more than he should. Every year, he moved his event to a new city and on several occasions changed the name. This didn't help his business; rather, it baffled his customers, who weren't sure if the newly named event was the same or different from the one they attended or heard about the previous year. Our colleague may simply have been trying to "get it right," but before too long his brand was a confused mess in customers' minds.

Have the courage to change, but also have the courage to retain what's *good* about your partnerships, businesses, or products. Above all, never change for the sake of change. Change for the sake of keeping things fresh and interesting.

WHEN THE SHEETS GET CHANGED FOR YOU

Imagine that you're a high-flying media executive in New York, enjoying life with your partner, who is also a successful executive. All of a sudden, a recession comes along and *bam*— you're both out of a job. That's a pretty massive "changing of the sheets" for a personal relationship. What do you do then? You don't curl up into a ball and give up. You muster even more courage and roll with it. If you're the Fabulous Beekman Boys, you even parlay it into an exciting new *business* partnership on, of all things, a goat farm.

In 2007 the Beekmans (Josh and Brent) purchased the historic Beekman 1802 farm in a Sharon Springs, New York, a bucolic village of 547 inhabitants (according to the 2000 census) near Albany. The two intended the property as a weekend place, and they imagined that they would spend many tranquil weekends together on the farm away from their hectic white-collar lives in New York City. It was not to be. In 2008, the two lost their jobs within a month of one another, casualties of the Great Recession. With their bank threatening to foreclose on their farm, the two came to a radical decision: They would give up their traditional careers (Josh had been a successful author and an advertising executive, Brent a Vice President at Martha Stewart's company, Martha Stewart Omnimedia) and make a go of it together on their farm, crafting soap and cheese using milk from a herd of goats.[30]

Many farmers make high-quality, artisanal products, but very few manage to create one of the nation's fastest growing lifestyle brands. That's exactly what the Beekmans have done. Putting their marketing chops to work, they set up an online store, the Beekman 1802 Mercantile, for their ever-expanding line of products created in collaboration with local artisans and farmers. Their website features a blog, recipes, and enticing imagery from the farm—all intended to enable others to "reconnect with real things," as Brent told the *New York Times*.

In 2009 and 2010, the Beekman Boys brought their story to prime time by starring in the reality TV show *The Fabulous Beekman Boys* on the Planet Green network. The show, depicting the joys and struggles of the Beekmans' adaptation to country life, became a huge favorite of Bob's. You can't believe how happy he was in 2012 when the Beekmans appeared on the show *The Amazing Race*—and won the million-dollar prize! He (and Jim, too) was even happier when the Beekmans generously contributed a video for us to show at our 2013 ALIS conference.

It's worth pausing to take stock of what the Beekmans have done. Here are two guys who suffered professional setbacks that commonly cause even the strongest personal partnerships to fall apart. Instead, they made the best of it, in the space of just five years launching a successful business, appearing on not one but two reality TV shows, and winning a million dollars. When we interviewed them during the summer of 2015, they were preparing for still more change, hiring on a new CEO to partner with them and help take their burgeoning business to the next level.

How did the Beekmans do it? Clearly they had business experience and talent, but most fundamentally they had the right *attitude* about change. Instead of looking at their layoffs as a disaster and falling into a depression, they saw them as a dramatic opportunity to "change the sheets." As they related, change sometimes happens to us, and sometimes we make it happen. Either way, the key is to have the courage to roll with both positive and negative change. "We lost our jobs," Josh said. "We didn't make that happen. We did start this crazy business, and then the first television show came along out of nowhere, and then *The Amazing Race* came out of nowhere. These things kept life fresh for us." Brent agreed, noting that their business had "grown very organically. It follows our life and then we follow it. I think we had some foundations to make a successful business, but by large we let the business take us where it wants to take us."

As the Beekmans tell it, they didn't panic in the face of adversity. After so many years working in corporate America, Josh had seen many clients who, becoming overly reliant on strategy and planning, weren't able to maneuver to meet changing circumstances. Determined to do better, he and Brent weren't afraid to entirely reinvent themselves. And that meant hunkering down and focusing on one step at a time, making the most of what they could control. "I think both of us just are really hard workers, and so we just set forth focusing on the things that needed to get done, and dividing and conquering." Even once they had developed a plan for their new business, the two made sure always to keep the door to change open and to stay flexible so as to meet whatever the business world or life might throw at them. And more recently, as their start-up has become established, they have had the luxury of proactively changing the sheets on occasion to keep things fresh. "When we get bored," Brent remarked, "we just look for whatever is going to change things up."[31]

NOT ONE PARTNERSHIP, BUT MANY

Late one night in 1980, while sitting in a tiny studio apartment in Paris and sipping wine, two aspiring young chefs made a pact. Someday, somehow, they would open a restaurant together. Months later, they both returned to the United States. One of them, Susan Feniger, headed to Los Angeles, while the other, Mary Sue Milliken, went to Chicago. Susan went back to work full-time at Ma Maison restaurant and also landed a part-time gig cooking in a tiny espresso bar some friends from l.a. Eyeworks had opened up.

The espresso bar was so small that Susan didn't have a traditional kitchen, just a hot plate and a couple of hibachis in the parking lot. There were exactly nine tables. None of this stopped Susan from creating, as her first dish, pickled veal tongue in a lobster sauce with pears. She was having fun and it occurred to her that this could be the opportunity that she and Mary Sue had been waiting for. After three months at the espresso bar, she called Mary Sue up and cajoled her into coming to Los Angeles.

A few months after that, the two officially went into business together in partnership with the original owners of the espresso bar. They named their place "City Café." Featuring cuisine from the south of France, the place was open from seven in the morning until midnight, serving breakfast, lunch, and dinner with the help of one employee. The two partners wrote the menu every day, depending on what their produce company and other vendors could deliver and what the women could find at local markets. "We were just having an amazing time," Susan told us. "We were working seven days a week, cooking out in the parking lot." And they were getting noticed, too. "At one point we were in the kitchen and we heard Julia Child's voice. She had come in to eat at our little tiny café that was basically serving all sorts of food that we had learned in all the various restaurants."

By 1982 Susan and Mary Sue felt the urge to incorporate new elements into their restaurant. Susan took a trip to India, and upon her return they began putting Indian-inspired dishes on the menu. Then Mary Sue went to Thailand, and they again expanded their repertoire. In 1985, with the café thriving, Susan and Mary Sue saw an opportunity to expand the business. With their two other business partners from l.a. Eyeworks, owners Barbara McReynolds and Gai Gherardi, they reopened City Café in a different, larger space as a full-service restaurant called "City Restaurant," installing a tandoori oven. They still had the tiny City Café space, but they weren't sure what to do with it. Eager to experiment with new flavors and cuisines, the two traveled to Mexico together and learned the culinary traditions of that country from the ground up. They stayed with a local family and spent each day going to markets, buying all kinds of ingredients to cook with. Driving a VW around Mexico, they tried every tiny taco stand they came across to learn even more. When they returned to Los Angeles, they took their initial City Café space and turned it into a concept called Border Grill, featuring a Mexican-inspired menu they had written themselves.

Border Grille was an incredible success that continues to this day. In 1990 the two business partners moved the restaurant to a larger location in Santa Monica. Since then, they've opened locations at Las Vegas's Mandalay Bay Resort and Casino, in downtown Los Angeles, at Los Angeles International

Airport, and at The Forum Shops at Caesars in Las Vegas, as well as two food trucks.

But all of this was only the beginning. During the 1990s, as Border Grill was taking off, Susan and Mary Sue started an entirely different career path as media personalities. In 1994 the pair took a red-eye to New York City and convinced a publisher to buy their first cookbook, *City Cuisine*. Then PBS called and asked them to do a show with Julia Child. A second cookbook followed, as well as a long-running show on the Food Network called "Too Hot Tamales." Oh, and a radio show on NPR called "Good Food." And three more cookbooks.

As Susan and Mary Sue will tell you, all of this experimentation helped keep their partnership fresh and fun. Mary Sue related, "For me, I get really bored and like to change my job every five or ten years, so I think part of keeping our partnership fresh was just to keep evolving our roles. Interestingly, as a result of me being restless and wanting to try new things, I think Susan has also developed that same restlessness." The changes in their business have also brought shifts in the nature of their working relationship. Originally, the two were joined at the hip, working side-by-side in the kitchen of the original City Café, communicating seamlessly and checking each other's work—a constant and delightful joint improvisation. As Mary Sue remembered, "We constantly did this dance where Susan would do the produce order and she'd leave the kitchen and I'd go check it to make sure she hadn't made any mistakes. Likewise, if I did the produce order, she would look at it. We basically did the exact same job all the time."

As their business has grown, however, systems and processes have arisen, as well as a clearer division of labor and more autonomy for each partner. Mary Sue now spends most of her time in the corporate office handling administrative tasks—legal issues, insurance, IT, finance. Susan has stayed in the kitchen (or rather, kitchens), traveling from restaurant to restaurant to meet with the staff and ensure that operations are running smoothly. Mary Sue focuses on stepping back and looking at the business in its entirety, while Susan immerses herself in the day-to-day intricacies. Both participate in regular meetings with executives to review operations and oversee marketing, and the two occasionally cook with one another. As Susan reflects, "Our partnership has changed pretty dramatically. We probably do way less stuff together than we ever did because we're not in the kitchen side-by-side. We started doing the same job, and our paths have come to form a kind of 'V,' yet our partnership is still incredibly strong. We have a lot more trust now and also comfort. I know what she's going to say, what seasonings she's going to use. We're one another's shadows."[32]

Most people think of a partnership as a single, unchanging thing. The truth is different and more nuanced. If you ask most people with longstanding relationships of ten, twenty, thirty years or more, you find that they don't have just *one* partnership over all that time. They reinvent their partnership in significant ways, sometimes more than once. They grow and adapt together as their business evolves and as external circumstances demand. They don't cling to any one particular way of doing things, any one style of interacting, any one definition of what their partnership is. Instead, they pay constant attention to how they're feeling about the business, and if their interest is waning or their daily routine feels stale, they change it up—usually *before* a crisis forces them to.

Our partnership hasn't survived because our initial business plan was somehow perfect, or because we're more talented or smarter than anyone else. The "we" in our lives has survived because we've been open to change and to critiquing our process to make it work for us. We've survived because time and again, in big ways and in small, we've changed the sheets.

LESSONS LEARNED

* *The most successful businesses and partnerships in the world can get complacent, stale and boring. Shake it up!*

* *As Google CEO Larry Page said, "You need to be a bit uncomfortable to stay relevant." We totally agree. Discomfort keeps you sharp.*

* *Adjusting the roles and responsibilities can bring new ideas, energy, and vitality to the partnership.*

* *Don't fear failure, embrace it.*

* *Sometimes the sheets get changed on you, and you have to adapt accordingly. It's not always a bad thing. As Johnny Mercer wrote, "accentuate the positive."*

CHAPTER THIRTEEN

Communicate, Negotiate, Capitulate

This book would not be complete without a recounting of one of our favorite stories of all time, what we affectionately call the penis conference story. In the early days Jim had a contract to organize a conference for another organization. He was working a full-time job, and this gig was a little something extra okay, a big extra he was doing on the side. Over the years, the conference grew to attract over 1,000 people each year, and the organization was making a lot of money on the event. Poor Jim, however, was making next to nothing—he had only a "stipend" to help cover his costs. This was fine at first, as the organization had noble plans to make a major impact in the hotel industry. Unfortunately, those plans never came to fruition, leaving Jim with a partnership that had fallen out of balance, and little to show for it.

By 2000 Jim was losing patience. He attempted to rebalance the relationship by asking for some additional money. The client balked, as his organization was already severely cutting budgets. Jim was starting to think hard about dropping the contract, quitting his day job, and going into business with Bob to produce similar events that we would own ourselves. We were talking about going out on our own, but neither one of us was sold on the idea quite yet. Jim had had this contract for a long time, and his day job was stable and paid well. Producing events on our own would entail significant financial risk and comprise a major change to our lives. Were we ready for the ups and downs of an entrepreneurial life?

Perhaps sensing that there was "trouble in paradise," the client decided to exercise more control over the event. Normally Jim (with Bob's help) hired the stage building crew and handled all design decisions, but that year, the organization announced that it would do this itself, leaving Jim to focus primarily on the event's content. *No problem*, we thought. We were not at all anxious for Jim to do much work if he wasn't properly compensated. As planning for the event progressed, we began to hear complaints from the new production company. They had either underbid the job or misunderstood the scope of work. With the production company's morale low, we wondered how successful the event would be. We were getting nervous.

On opening day of the 2001 event, we made our way to the venue, the hotel's grand ballroom. Delegates were filing in, and ushers were seating them for the opening session. The first panel was an impressive one, featuring the presidents and CEOs of the world's biggest hotel chains. A few minutes before the start of the show, these VIP speakers were seated on a stage built on a rotating turnstile. Initially, they were out of view to the audience; all spectators could see was a generic graphic on stage depicting a two-dimensional cityscape. The plan was that as the stage rotated, the cityscape would move out of view and the speakers would come face-to-face with the audience while sitting in front of a space ship that conveyed the conference's futuristic "theme," which played off of the film "2001: A Space Odyssey." Clever, right?

The lights dimmed and dramatic space-sounding music played over the sound system. The stage began to rotate, and the hospitality executives came into view, seated directly under the spaceship. And what a rocket it was. It looked—if you can picture it—like a giant, pink-headed penis, with two "fuel tanks" on either side. From close up, it was hard to see the resemblance. But from the audience perspective, with proper lighting, there was no mistaking the anatomical likeness. There was a giant penis on stage.

Audience members let out gasps, which turned to chuckles, which turned to laughter. The presidents and CEOs smiled and nodded, "pleased" with their dramatic entrance and boisterous crowd response. They had no clue that they were sitting under a giant "dick," which made us, the organizers look like "dicks." The production company, working under tight budget restrictions in a less-than-pleasant relationship, appeared to have gotten their revenge.

As we sat in the audience watching this unfold, the two of us looked at one another in shock. "Are you thinking what I'm thinking?" Bob said to Jim. Jim nodded his head. It was decided: Jim couldn't collaborate with this client any longer; he had struggled long enough with a partnership that wasn't working for him. It was time for us to move on and do our own thing together, as proper business partners. We didn't know how or when, but we would make it happen. It's hard enough working in a dysfunctional partnership, but this one was embarrassing us professionally.

Conflict and differences of opinion arise in even the most successful and longstanding of partnerships. Sometimes a partner feels miffed by a perceived insensitivity or an imbalance that just won't go away. Other times it's infidelity, loss of interest, a shift in a partner's goals and priorities, disagreement about the strategic direction, mistrust engendered by poor communication, or a combination of these. Although you might have taken great care setting up the partnership, enshrining your arrangement in the finest legal documents, sometimes things just don't go smoothly.

That's not to say conflict or tension always results in a giant penis blasting across a stage. Most of the time you can work things out, especially if mutual respect still exists among the partners. The key is to recognize the warning signs and talk through the issues. We believe that partnerships usually fall apart when communication breaks down and partners grow apart and lose respect for each other. In every conflict situation we've been in, we've done our best to listen, compromise, and even comfortably capitulate on points being raised by our partners. In a few situations, no amount of communication, negotiation, or capitulation made a problematic partnership work for us, so we were forced to "divorce." But as we've found, even that sad outcome has usually worked out well. Some of the best, most lucrative things we are doing today are the result of epiphanies in prior partnerships, "aha" moments when we realized our destinies were no longer linked.

AVOIDING PHALLIC FIASCOS

Of course, we far prefer to prevent ruptures that destroy otherwise successful partnerships. As we've found, it pays to stay alert and work hard to keep small conflicts or tensions from raging out of control. The first twelve chapters of this book can help with that; the partnership principles we've presented up until now convey lessons we've learned that help us either avoid conflict entirely or quickly dispose of it when it does emerge (but before it can become deadly!).

Think about it: If you take your time choosing the right partner for the right reasons, if you know yourself well, and if you stay true to your values and goals and DGIA (chapters 1–4), you'll be avoiding many potential sources of conflict that arise when people rush thoughtlessly into relationships.

Crafting a partnership playbook and committing to it fully (chapters 5 and 6) allows you to avoid all those time-wasting petty disputes around who is supposed to do what. Strategize properly about your business (chapter 7), and you'll stand a better chance of your venture succeeding, avoiding the tensions that often arise when businesses flounder.

That's not all. If you play it straight even when it's tough (chapter 8), you'll build mutual trust and respect even in the face of challenges that might otherwise pit partners against one another. Prioritizing face time (chapter 9) allows you to understand one another better, reducing miscommunications that commonly lead to disputes and fights. Giving back and sharing your success (chapter 10) binds you together in a positive way around a larger purpose, which allows you to put small disputes into perspective. Maintaining balance (chapter 11) prevents a range of resentments that blow up over time when one partner is doing or getting more than the other. Finally, changing the sheets (chapter 12) helps circumvent the stasis that can lead to dissatisfaction, disillusionment, and eventually, pitched battle between partners.

In sum, the partnership principles in this book have allowed us to communicate well and also maintain flexibility, fluidity, and fun in the relationship; these in turn have led us to value the relationships more and make extra effort to resolve conflict. It isn't rocket science: When partners consistently feel welcome, appreciated, listened to, understood, and respected, they get along better. They tend not to sweat the small stuff as much—and they realize that almost all of it *is* small stuff.

READ THE SIGNS

Applying the partnership principles does not guarantee that a partnership won't eventually fall apart. In dealing with external partners, we've had some fatal conflicts over the years, some requiring lawyers. For this reason, even as we try to stay true to our own principles, we also stay on the lookout for warning signs that conflict is festering below the surface. We ask ourselves:

+ When we bring up a problem or issue, is our partner consistently annoyed or on the defensive?

+ Does the same problem or issue keep coming up in our partnership, despite previous conversations?

+ In situations when we have multiple partners, are they taking sides over issues in predictable ways?

+ Are employees routinely showing disrespect for one partner or the other?

+ Is gossip running rampant around the office?

+ Have partners seemed to have "given up" on the business? Is there a palpable lack of enthusiasm?

+ Is performance consistently off or stagnant, yet nobody wants to talk about why?

+ Do partners keep trying to buy or develop new business ideas rather than fix existing problems?

+ Do some partners want to grow while others are content to keep things the same?

These signs don't necessarily "prove" that conflict is festering, but in our experience they're a pretty good indication. If one of these signs exists in your partnership, pay closer attention: you may have something to worry about. If two or more of them appear, you and your partners are probably experiencing some significant conflict, and you should sit down *soon* to work it out. If all of these signs are present, then break out the defibrillator paddles—chances are, the partnership needs a powerful jolt.

WIFE-GATE

In most conflict situations, simply airing out the issues can allow you to make headway, even quickly resolve problems. As *The Amazing Race* co-creator and executive producer Elise Doganieri told us, the one quality that characterized winning teams on the show was their superior ability to communicate. "The thing that I see is that they listen to each other, and not only do they listen, but they allow both partners to have their way. They take turns. They share. They let each other explore their thoughts. There's a mutual respect for each other's ideas, and it is a respect for each other."[33] Conversely, those teams that don't do well have trouble communicating in difficult times. When one partners speaks, the other doesn't listen, and so the partner who is speaking doesn't feel heard. Rather than resolving conflict, they only ramp it up further.

Elise further related that she and her partner Bertram had become much more skilled themselves over time at communicating in conflict situations. "I used to jump right in, but now I really wait for the right moment to talk about it, and we have learned the dance around each other, to negotiate certain outcomes that we both want. He knows how to speak to me in a certain way, and I know how to speak to him in a certain way where we can both hear each other."[34] The two also make sure always to do this "dance" behind closed doors, so that they can speak honestly with one another and maintain a common front for their employees.

What if you haven't known your partner for decades? The good news is that you can still find ways to work though conflict together effectively. Consider an episode from our business that we affectionately call "Wife-gate." At one of the events we produced, our partner found himself in a tight spot when some of his male colleagues wanted to bring their wives to our event's cocktail party without paying for tickets. We have a longstanding policy of giving each partner a specific number of complimentary guest registrations for each event. In this case, our partner had already used up all of his comps.

Our partner couldn't bring himself to say no to his colleagues, so he quietly added their wives' names to the official list of delegates, hoping we wouldn't notice. We didn't notice at first—it's an event with thousands of attendees—but then we spotted several of the wives at the cocktail reception. This put us in a difficult spot. We had already told some of our own colleagues and major sponsors that they couldn't bring their wives and significant others. It had been awkward to do that, but we felt obligated to follow the rules and treat everyone equally. We felt angry that our partner hadn't played by the rules. It wasn't fair to us, nor was it fair to all the other delegates, sponsors, and supporters whose spouses were told no.

We were in conflict with our partner, and we had to do something about it. After the event, we sat down with him to talk it out. He described to us the pressures he was under, and he said he felt he had no choice but to bend—his colleagues expected special treatment. "Yes," we said, "we get it, but we say no to attendees, sponsors, and friends every day when they ask for favors." We explained to him our philosophy of being "Switzerland"—entirely neutral and fair—and we further explained how this philosophy benefited our business over the long term. At first, our partner didn't agree with our position, but after a few conversations, heated at times, he came to understand that in pursuing fairness, we really were doing what was best for the partnership. He agreed never to repeat Wife-gate, and we resolved the problem before it threatened our entire working relationship.

IS IT A BOULDER OR A PEBBLE?

In this case, our partner capitulated, but in other cases, we've had to give in. At another event we produce, we found ourselves at odds with our partners over design decisions. When it came to the promotional brochure, our partner, who fancies himself as the arbiter of good taste, would only use the colors grey and red. Yellow? No. Blue? No. Just grey and red. The logo was another point of conflict: we just could not find a design on which the partners could all agree. Weeks went by, then months, and we still hadn't come to consensus. Eventually, we were so exhausted that we just gave way. The final marketing piece wasn't the best it could be in our opinion, but at least the partnership was intact.

How do you know when to capitulate and when to stand firm and possibly terminate a relationship that isn't working? Although hard-and-fast rules don't exist, we have some general guidelines that work for us. We usually won't capitulate when:

- ✦ It means compromising our core values, which makes it hard for us to look at ourselves in the mirror.

- ✦ It will undermine the foundation of our business model.

- ✦ It will have potentially severe long-term consequences.

- ✦ It will cost us the respect of our partner or our customers.

- ✦ It represents only a short-term fix to a problem, not a long-term solution.

+ It is the only option we've considered and we haven't
   yet taken the time to really study the problem.

Wife-gate *did* undermine both our business model and our
values. Giving away tickets was a short-term fix, and our partner would have lost respect for us if we'd failed to respond to
his subterfuge. For those reasons, we stood firm. As for the
design decisions, those ultimately didn't go against our core
values, nor did it affect our business model, so we were more
willing to let our partner prevail.

Whenever we're tempted to take a hard stand, we always
cast a critical eye on ourselves. Are we digging in our heels
out of ego or stubbornness? Does our partner know more about
this subject than we do? Are there alternatives that neither of
us has considered yet? Is the issue really worth risking the
partnership?

When a conflict proves especially vexing, we go deeper,
stepping away and asking ourselves how much the issue at
hand truly matters to us, based on gut feelings. We fell into the
habit of taking a more intuitive approach in these situations
after a painful unraveling of one of our business ventures. We
had joined up with a group of partners to create one of the finest hospitality events in the world. Over time, the partnership
changed; some partners became less motivated to participate,
one was sold to someone else, and new partners joined the
team. The arrangement still worked for a while, but the original
chemistry and shared vision was lost. Disagreements emerged
as well as well as finger pointing, turf grabbing, second-guess-
ing, saber rattling, and unilateral behavior. You name it; it was
a mess. An ugly and expensive court battle loomed.

Having helped put the partnership together in the first
place, we were devastated to see it disintegrate. The failure
felt personal to us, and we couldn't stop stressing over it. We

suffered through months of sleepless nights and unproductive days. Eventually—and this is how bad it got—we consulted Jim's older sister Jeanne, a psychic and "old soul," as well as a mystic friend of hers named Jan, about what we should do. Jan went deep into herself and channeled what she called "the Brotherhood," a higher level of consciousness, spirit, or soul.

The feedback from the Brotherhood was blunt and to the point. We were experiencing torment because we were choosing to make the conflict a "boulder" in the road and not a "pebble." If instead we viewed it as a "pebble," or an obstacle we could just step over or kick out of the way, our perspective would change. Hmm . . . that actually made some pretty good sense. We shifted the way we saw the situation, removing our energy from the conflict. And what do you know, it worked! Our new perspective allowed us to come to a settlement more easily with our partners and move on. The partnership was over, but we never looked back. We quickly and easily turned to focus on more positive parts of our business, saving a ton on legal fees. It was nice to get a good night sleep again for a change.

In the heat of conflict, try stepping back and asking yourself if you're staring at a boulder, or if it's simply a pebble that *seems* like a boulder. Nine times out of ten, it's a pebble, but because you're emotionally connected to the conflict, it can feel much bigger.

GETTING OUTSIDE HELP

In 2005 restaurateurs Susan Feninger and Mary Sue Milliken faced a crisis, one of the most difficult their partnership had ever seen. The two had been on an incredible ride together for almost three decades. They were like family, their personal and professional lives intricately intertwined. In fact, after Susan came out as a lesbian, Mary Sue had married Susan's ex-husband! Yet as the growth of their businesses slowed, it seemed as if the two had drifted apart and formed different goals and priorities. Susan wanted to grow the company as much as ever; she wanted to get out there and continue to open new restaurant concepts. Mary Sue wanted to slow down; unlike Susan, she had two kids, and she wanted to be home with them every night.

Susan grew increasingly frustrated, and tension mounted. The two didn't know what to do. They didn't want to end their partnership, but they also didn't see a way forward. Susan was afraid that if something didn't change, she would begin to resent Mary Sue. Finally, the two did what thousands of couples do when in hard times: They went to therapy.

Yes, therapy.

Meeting with a counselor over a period of months, Susan and Mary Sue explored their feelings more deeply than they ever had before, talking about their shared history, their current situation, and the options available to them. Eventually, they decided to remain business partners, but for the first time ever, they would each feel free to pursue their own, independent ventures as well. In 2009, Susan opened up a new restaurant called Street, independently from Border Grill, with new partner Kajsa Alger. In 2013, Susan and Kajsa remodeled Street and reopened as Mud Hen Tavern, which in 2014 added Blue Window, an innovative take-out window food stop that completely changes concept every six months. During our conversation, Susan credited Mary Sue's willingness to communicate as the reason their partnership was able to survive. "Mary Sue was incredibly brave. Thanks to our time in therapy, she just got it, and we were able to make this transition with little conflict. I mean, we had never done anything separately before. All our media interviews we did together. All our TV shows, too. Now, suddenly, I was doing interviews for Street without Mary

Sue. I'm sure she had to deal with emotional stuff. We just got through it."

When we sat down with Mary Sue, she emphasized the value of soliciting advice from all kinds of people outside the partnership. "It's important to keep the lines of communication open, but when we get really stuck, we also have a great kitchen cabinet of advisors we can bring in. It's good to get outside perspective, because when you've been a partner for over thirty years, you can get kind of clouded or heated or emotional in a way that isn't really about the issue anymore."[35]

Psychics, therapists, attorneys—we find that outside sources make all the difference when a partnership is on the line and you need to figure out what to do. These outsiders might not give you *"the* answer," but they can at least help you become more aware of your own behavior. Before we capitulate on a potentially important issue or write off a partnership as a lost cause and decapitate it, we always try to cogitate with at least one outsider, usually another experienced entrepreneur, consultant friends, or our legal counsel (we save the psychic for those truly desperate situations). Partnerships are important to us, so when we decide their fate, we want to make sure we've looked at the problem from every angle, and looked deep within ourselves, too.

If you've consulted a trusted advisor, searched your soul in therapy, and still feel it necessary to end the partnership, make sure you do it with the same respect and care you applied in making the decision. On at least three occasions now, we've ended longstanding external partnerships, and each time we've managed to do it in an amicable way, without burning any bridges. It's not that we weren't upset or emotional; we were. But we were determined to behave strategically, keeping the door at least partially open for future collaboration. The way we look at it, industries are often much smaller than they appear; you never know if an opportunity will arise and a renewed partnership might make sense later on. In fact, as of this writing, we've had conversations with all three of our former partners about working together in the future. When breaking off a partnership, we've tried to regard it optimistically not as the end, but as a pregnant pause before whatever may come next.

DON'T FORGET TO CELEBRATE

In 2012 we looked back at all the conferences we had produced and realized something pretty cool: We were about to create our 100th event.

Where had the time gone? Had we really done 100 events??

Indeed we had. We decided we needed to find a way to recognize many of the external partners, sponsors, and other special people in our lives who helped make this success possible. We wanted to throw a special party to say thanks, and since our 100th event would be held in London, we wanted this party to be extremely British. We challenged ourselves to create a blowout event, something people would remember for years. After all, producing spectacular shows is what we do.

As we've mentioned, Bob is a member of the Clan Hay of Scotland. In point of fact, he is the feudal Baron of Delgaty, a small area in Northeast Scotland, outside Aberdeen, that has ties to Clan Hay. The chief of the Clan is the Earl of Erroll, a member of The House of Lords. Bob had connected with His Lordship a couple years earlier when Lord Erroll invited us to tea at Parliament. We wondered: Could His Lordship help us put together an event in Britain's Parliament building? Lord Erroll informed us that some rooms in the Parliament building were used for private functions, and His Lordship was willing to help us arrange a private event for our group.

Talk about special. We wound up holding an intimate cocktail party—just sixty guests—in the Attlee Room, a small but stunning space located in the far southwest corner of the House of Lords wing of the Parliament building. The room was steeped in history, decorated with intricate wood paneling and antique Victorian furniture. As our guests filtered in, His Lordship, who had generously agreed to host the event, stood waiting in the entryway to greet them personally. They arrived wide-eyed, having just passed through Parliament's tight security.

When everyone had arrived, His Lordship offered opening remarks, and our guests chatted with him and mingled with one another. We thought the party was going great, but apparently it was just getting started. To our surprise, His Lordship offered to give guests private tours of Parliament. Remember, this was in the evening. It was dark, and Parliament was closed to the public—but not to His Lordship. He escorted our party through the various rooms of the House of Lords, flipping the light switches on as he went. Imagine how thrilling it would be to have the White House or the Capitol Building in Washington DC at your disposal, with nobody else around. That's what this was like. We passed portraits of notable British politicians and sovereigns, including His Lordship's ancestor, King William IV. The highlight was seeing Her Majesty the Queen's throne in the House of Lords chamber. To Bob's horror, Jim was tempted to sit on it, but in the end he didn't break protocol.

As we made our way back to the Attlee Room after the tour, His Lordship had another idea. A "secret" terrace at the back of the Lord's wing of Parliament offered a "brilliant" view of the Thames River. Through the back hallways of the Lord's wing we went, champagne flutes in hand. We passed through a non-descript door and onto a private terrace overlooking the Thames. Floodlights positioned along the Thames were trained on the Parliament building, and as we stood there, they illuminated us all in what we can only describe as an aura of awe.

We had all seen the Parliament building before at night, but always from across the river. Now we were part of the spectacle—up-close and personal. And that view of the Thames was indeed "brilliant."

All too soon, Lord Erroll rounded us up and took us back to the Attlee Room, where we said our goodbyes. Our guests thanked us *profusely* for arranging such a special event just for them. As they filed out, we handed them each a gift bag of chocolates and champagne affixed with the special label of the House of Lords. If memory serves, His Lordship took hold of one himself before he dashed.

We gathered up the leftover champagne and chocolates and distributed it to the servers and security guards who had worked at the party. As we left the House of Lords, all our guests had smiles on their faces, and so did we. What a celebration!

If you're together with a partner long enough, you're going to experience some tough times. Yet the most successful partnerships weather these storms, simply because each partner respects, admires, trusts, and just plain *likes* the other enough to stick it out. As Mary Sue told us, there had been "plenty of times" over the years when she questioned her partnership. "At these times, I've looked at it and weighed the positive and negative, and I've always decided that I still wanted be a partner, and that I wanted to be *her* partner. I think our partnership is much stronger today because it went through these moments when one of us was really questioning it."

Similarly, Mitchell Gold told us of how he maintained a strong business relationship with partner Bob Williams even though the two had ended their romantic partnership and found other mates. When we marveled at how hard that must have been, Mitchell confirmed that the transition wasn't easy; sometimes tensions flared at the office. Yet the two worked through it, in large part because of their mutual respect. "I think it comes down to respect," he said. "If I didn't think Bob was talented and smart and a good person, I would have gotten myself out of our business partnership. To this day, Bob is my biggest cheerleader. If I'm giving a speech, he's the one hugging me and telling me I did great. We remain good friends, and we socialize together with our life partners as couples. We just love one another. We really do."[36]

When you've been through the ups and downs of a relationship, when you've tested your partnership and found it to be strong, there's one more thing you need to do: celebrate it. We take the task of celebrating so seriously that we build it into our business ventures, and we also regularly celebrate our informal partnerships. At our Hong Kong event, one of our partners has taken it on himself to coordinate a dinner party each year for our business partners and key supporters, toasting our continued success. Our ALIS summer sessions, described in the last chapter, are partly marketing vehicles for us, but they likewise allow us to celebrate the delegates who attend our event and thank them for their support.

Partnerships that succeed over the long term are not easy, and so many people in business (and in life) can't make them last. If you've suffered through those tensions and difficult conversations with partners, and your relationships have prevailed—that's worth celebrating. Even if you've only *just* started your partnership and have managed to make it through the first year, that's still worth celebrating. It's important to share the joys of your partnership with one another. By celebrating what we have achieved together, we set ourselves up for even greater accomplishments in the future. We remind ourselves that together, we can do anything.

LESSONS LEARNED

* *Small disagreements can grow into larger conflicts if left unaddressed.*

* *Is it a pebble or a boulder? It's all about perspective and how partners approach a conflict.*

* *Picking the right partner at the beginning goes a long way toward minimizing the potential for conflict down the line.*

* *Strong, transparent communication between partners is perhaps the most important protection against damaging conflict.*

* *Don't be afraid to ask for outside help if internal conflict is jeopardizing your partnership.*

* *Don't forget to celebrate the wins, big and small!*

The Greatest Celebration
of All

Nokia Theatre[37] in Los Angeles, site of our signature ALIS hotel investment conference, is a vast space with seating for more than 7,000. Typically Jim stands on stage during the event and looks out at a sea of faces. On one afternoon in July 2014, the theater stood empty with just the house lights on. The only people present were the two of us and a few close friends. We were putting on yet another show, but this one was different from the rest. We had come to this familiar stage to mark an important milestone in our partnership, and also to reflect on over twenty years of battles we'd helped fight for a cause that mattered greatly to us.

Right after the two of us met in 1991, we became active supporters of the gay rights movement. Never in a million years did we imagine that we would be able to live together in the United States as a married couple. But we got involved anyway, helping to build the chapter of the Human Rights Campaign (HRC) in Orange County, California, a place where it was very difficult to live openly as gay men. We continued to support HRC over the years, not only giving money but also attending meetings and organizing events, some of them held in our home. Over and over again, we vowed to continue this important work, hoping that future generations of LGBT people would achieve the equality that our friends and us, sadly, hadn't enjoyed.

On June 26, 2013, the unthinkable happened: The Defense of Marriage Act (DOMA) and Proposition 8 were overturned by the United States Supreme Court. As a result, it finally became possible for the two of us to get legally married in the state of California, with federal recognition of the union. When we watched the scene unfold on television, we couldn't hold back the tears. We recalled all the hard work that so many people had contributed over so many years, and we remembered as well our many friends who had succumbed to AIDS and hadn't lived to see this day.

As the impact of the Supreme Court ruling sank in, we began to ask ourselves whether we wanted to get married. We weren't sure. Although we'd fought for equality, we didn't know whether we ourselves needed a legal ceremony in order to feel committed to one another. We finally realized that we *had* to get married, not just for us, but to honor all those who worked so hard over the decades for our rights. Marriage wasn't just a piece of paper; the right to marry represented a major accomplishment of ours, and a gift that other LGBT people working alongside us had given us.

So there we were in that softly lighted theater on July 21, 2014, joining together in matrimony. It felt surreal standing there on that huge stage with a simple spotlight shining down on us; we felt like we were in our own universe, the only people alive in the world, tiny and insignificant. As we said the words that made us husband and husband, we felt that we had come to the end of a decades-long journey. It meant a lot that the officiant, John Duran, had been at the cocktail party where we had met twenty-five years earlier. When Jim rebuffed Bob at first, Duran was the one who encouraged Jim to try again to strike up a conversation.

How *have* we managed to stick together for so long without killing one another? How have we worked side by side in the business and made it the powerhouse that it is today? The partnership principles presented in this book are our answer. And yet, during the months we spent researching and writing this book, we found that a deeper answer was also emerging. Underlying all of our principles, we discovered, is a simple message: *Take partnerships seriously. Work hard to make them work. Never take them for granted.*

In the end, succeeding with partnership is not a matter of specific practices, but of an abiding attitude of trust, respect, commitment, and for us, love. Partnerships are a big deal—not just specific partnerships, but the very *idea* of partnership. That's why, from the very inception of a relationship, partners should proceed slowly, cautiously, thoughtfully, going "all in," and doing whatever they can to keep the relationship vibrant and healthy. They should honor their relationship at every turn and with all their strength.

Partnership is the most important thing in our lives. The way we look at it, life is a journey, and who wants to go through it alone, floating aimlessly like rocks in space? We wouldn't. Life and work is much more fun and meaningful when we do it *with* someone else—when our trajectories run closely in parallel. Our constant quest for togetherness, we think, has been our ultimate secret to success. We'll do whatever it takes to make any of our partnerships great. Over time, through many crises and mistakes, that commitment has allowed us not merely to survive intact; it has also led us to devise our principles, which in turn have helped us make our partnerships thrive.

So many people admire long-term partnerships. We sensed as much from the outpouring of congratulations we received when posting news of our wedding on social media. We received hundreds of likes and comments from friends, relatives, business associates, and acquaintances both gay and straight, including some we didn't know all that well. The response was overwhelming and affirming. But as we have also seen first-hand, many people struggle to maintain partnerships. The principles in this book provide some guidance, but if you're struggling, we would ask you to peer closely into your heart. How important are partnerships to you, really? Are you ready to commit to them in the fullest sense? Do your actions match up to this professed commitment? Really, anybody can sustain partnerships over time—it's not rocket science—but it does take the right attitude. What's yours? If partnerships don't matter most of all to you, what does?

That day in the Nokia Theatre, we were not merely looking backward in time; we were also launching a new phase in our partnership. We were heading toward a special time in our lives—not retirement, but a time when we'll need to slow down a bit, move away from our core business and work on other projects we're passionate about. We anticipated that the going wouldn't always be easy, but we took comfort in knowing that we were both still "all in" and that during tough times we would have our principles to guide us. We hope that this book offers you similar comfort and guidance as you pursue your own partnership journeys. Relish the fact that for some miraculous reason, your and your partner's trajectories collided, and that you're now floating together in this great big universe. Make the most of your time together. Enjoy it. Push through the difficulties. Go all in. You might not always get it right, but may you learn from your mistakes and become, over time, the very smartest of partners.

Endnotes

1. "Coke Purchasing Merv Griffin Unit," *The New York Times*, February 1986, http://www.nytimes.com/1986/02/19/business/coke-purchasing-merv-griffin-unit.html.

2. Saulny, Susan, "Businessmen Who Created Fashion Cafe Are Hit With Fraud Charges," *The New York Times*, December 12, 2000, http://www.nytimes.com/2000/12/12/nyregion/businessmen-who-created-fashion-cafe-are-hit-with-fraud-charges.html.

3. Mathews, Ross. *Man Up! Tales of My Delusional Self-Confidence*. (New York: Grand Central, 2013) p. 23.

4. Perman, Stacy, "Famous Business Partnerships—Bill Hewlett and David Packard," *Bloomberg Business*, November 21, 2008, http://www.bloomberg.com/ss/00/11/1121_famous_partnerships/6.htm.

5. Interview with Elise Doganieri, August 8, 2015.

6. Marston, William. *Emotions of Normal People*. (Routledge, Trench, Trubner & Co., Ltd. 1928).

7. Our discussion of DISC reproduces portions of an article we wrote for *The Advocate*. Jim Burba and Bob Hayes, "Op-ed: How to Succeed in Business—With Your Partner," *The Advocate*, January 11, 2013, http://www.advocate.com/commentary/2013/01/11/how-succeed-business-your-partner.

8. Interview with Mitchell Gold, July 2, 2015.

9. Interview with Tom Corcoran, April 22, 2015.

10. Interview with Trina Turk and Jonathan Skow, June 3, 2015.

11. Williams, Tim, "Defining Partner Roles and Responsibilities," *Ignition Consulting Group*, April 23, 2010, http://www.ignitiongroup.com/guide/defining-partner-roles-and-responsibilities/.

12. Interview with Tom Corcoran, April 22, 2015.

13. Interview with Elise Doganieri, August 8, 2015.

14. Interview with Tom Corcoran, April 22, 2015.

15. Interview with Trina Turk and Jonathan Skow, June 3, 2015.

16. Interview with Mitchell Gold, July 2, 2015.

17. Lin, Helen, "How Your Cell Phone Hurts Your Relationships," *Scientific American*, September 4, 2012, http://www.scientificamerican.com/article/how-your-cell-phone-hurts-your-relationships/.

18. Jacinto, Jill, "5 Reasons Millennials Actually Prefer Talking Face-to-Face," *Millennial Magazine*, December 1, 2014, http://millennialmagazine.com/5-reasons-millennials-actually-prefer-talking-face-to-face/.

19. Pulled from http://www.youthcareerinitiative.org/.

20. Interview with Ivanka Trump, May 17, 2015.

21. Interview with Trina Turk and Jonathan Skow, June 3, 2015.

22. Interview with Jonathan Tisch, July 10, 2015.

23. Interview with Gavin and Hilary Newsom, July 29, 2015.

24. Interview with Gavin and Hilary Newsom, July 29, 2015.

25. Interview with Jonathan Tisch, July 10, 2015.

26. Interview with Jonathan Tisch, July 10, 2015.

27. Lien, Tracey, "Google, coming to grips with its giant size, forms a parent company: Alphabet," *Los Angeles Times*, August 10, 2015, http://www.latimes.com/business/la-fi-google-alphabet-20150810-story.html.

28. Interview with Gavin and Hilary Newsom, July 29, 2015.

29. J. Willard Marriott, January 20, 1964.

30. Pulled from http://beekman1802.com/.

31. Interview with the Beekman Boys, August 14, 2015.

32. Interview with Mary Sue Milliken, August 6, 2015, and Susan Feniger, July 29, 2015.

33. Interview with Elise Doganieri, August 8, 2015.

34. Interview with Elise Doganieri, August 8, 2015.

35. Interview with Mary Sue Milliken, August 6, 2015, and Susan Feniger, July 29, 2015.

36. Interview with Mitchell Gold, July 2, 2015.

37. Renamed Microsoft Theater on June 9, 2015.

About the Authors

PHOTOGRAPH © JANA CRUDER

JIM BURBA AND BOB HAYES have been successful life partners for more than 25 years and business partners for more than 15 years. Cofounders of Burba Hotel Network (BHN), the couple develops and produces the world's most prominent conferences for the hotel investment community. BHN was founded on the principle of sharing success, and its events have generated more than US $15 million for scholarships, education, and social services organizations.

In 2013 the duo formed Burba Hayes LLC, an entertainment production company. Their first film *Space Station 76* debuted in 2014 at the SXSW Film Festival in Austin, Texas, and was the closing gala film at Outfest 2014 in Los Angeles. Their Broadway musical *Disaster!* ran on Broadway in early 2016. More films and a reality TV show are in the works.

Jim Burba is a member of the International Society of Hospitality Consultants (ISHC) and the Industry Real Estate Advisory Council (IREFAC). In 2007 California Governor Arnold Schwarzenegger appointed Burba to a second term on the California Travel & Tourism Commission. He received an MBA in business and marketing from UCLA and his BA in from the School of Hospitality Business at Michigan State University.

Bob Hayes is a political science graduate of California State University Fullerton; he is a past instructor for UCLA Extension in real estate investment, an award winning real estate sales professional, an entrepreneur, and an avid history buff.

Together, Burba and Hayes have contributed their expertise in articles for *HOTELS' Investment Outlook, Travel Weekly*, Advocate.com, Outtraveler.com, and *Successful Meetings*. They are contributors and editorial board members for *California Meetings and Events* magazine.

For four years running, Burba and Hayes have been named by *Out Magazine* as one of the "Power Couples to Know" along with luminaries and their life partners, including clothing designer Tom Ford, singer Sir Elton John, and talk show host Ellen DeGeneres.

For more information about Burba Hotel Network and *Smart Partners* please visit: www.BurbaHayes.com